Hill & Redman's
Law of Landlord and Tenant

Residential Tenancies Precedents

Special Bulletin

Publishing Manager
Vazken Davidian

Issue Editor
Jenny Kallin

Hill & Redman's
Law of Landlord and Tenant

Residential Tenancies Precedents

Special Bulletin

Emma Copestake
Solicitor, Farrer & Co

John Furber QC
General Editor

LexisNexis™ UK

Members of the LexisNexis Group worldwide

United Kingdom	LexisNexis UK, a Division of Reed Elsevier (UK) Ltd, Halsbury House, 35 Chancery Lane, LONDON, WC2A 1EL, and 4 Hill Street, EDINBURGH EH2 3JZ
Argentina	LexisNexis Argentina, BUENOS AIRES
Australia	LexisNexis Butterworths, CHATSWOOD, New South Wales
Austria	LexisNexis Verlag ARD Orac GmbH & Co KG, VIENNA
Canada	LexisNexis Butterworths, MARKHAM, Ontario
Chile	LexisNexis Chile Ltda, SANTIAGO DE CHILE
Czech Republic	Nakladatelství Orac sro, PRAGUE
France	Editions du Juris-Classeur SA, PARIS
Germany	LexisNexis Deutschland GmbH, FRANKFURT, MUNSTER
Hong Kong	LexisNexis Butterworths, HONG KONG
Hungary	HVG-Orac, BUDAPEST
India	LexisNexis Butterworths, NEW DELHI
Ireland	Butterworths (Ireland) Ltd, DUBLIN
Italy	Giuffrè Editore, MILAN
Malaysia	Malayan Law Journal Sdn Bhd, KUALA LUMPUR
New Zealand	LexisNexis Butterworths, WELLINGTON
Poland	Wydawnictwo Prawnicze LexisNexis, WARSAW
Singapore	LexisNexis Butterworths, SINGAPORE
South Africa	LexisNexis Butterworths, DURBAN
Switzerland	Stämpfli Verlag AG, BERNE
USA	LexisNexis, DAYTON, Ohio

© Reed Elsevier (UK) Ltd 2003

A CIP Catalogue record for this book is available from the British Library.

ISBN 0 406 97410 1

Typeset by Columns Design Ltd, Reading, Berks
Printed and bound in Great Britain by CPI (Bath)

Visit LexisNexis UK at www.lexisnexis.co.uk

Contents

Contents

Table of Statutes

Table of Statutory Instruments

All entries refer to page number

Table of Cases

All entries refer to page number

Form 1
Assured shorthold tenancy agreement for a fixed term suitable for house or flat [1]

TAKE NOTICE THAT THIS TENANCY AGREEMENT IS A BINDING DOCUMENT. BEFORE SIGNING IT YOU SHOULD READ IT CAREFULLY TO ENSURE THAT IT CONTAINS EVERYTHING YOU DO WANT AND NOTHING THAT IS UNACCEPTABLE TO YOU [2]

THIS AGREEMENT is made the   day of   [   ]

BETWEEN

(1)   [   ] [company Registration Number] [of
     [   ] *OR* whose registered office is at
     [   ]] ('the Landlord') [and whose address
     for service in England and Wales is at [   ][3]]

(2)   [   ] of [   ] ('the Tenant')

[1.1]

1. Definitions

'the Agent' means [   ] of [   ][4]

['the Building' means the building known as [   ] of which
     the Premises form part][5]

'the Deposit' means the sum of £[   ]

['the Headlease' means the lease dated [   ] and made
     between [   ] (1) and [   ] (2)][6]

'the Inventory' means the list of [furniture, furnishings] fixtures and other
     items in the Premises which will be signed by both parties prior to
     commencement of the Term and which records their present state
     and condition

'the Premises' means [[the flat numbered [   ] on the
     [   ] floor at the Building] *OR* [the house known
     as [   ]] [shown for identification purposes only
     edged [red] on the plan annexed to this Agreement]

'the Rent' means £[   ] a [year *OR* month *OR* week][7]

'the Term' [   ] from and including [   ]
and any period of holding over or extension or continuance by
statute or common law[8]

[1.2]

2. Interpretation

2.1   Wherever the context so admits the expression 'the Landlord'
includes the person for the time being entitled to the reversion
immediately expectant on the determination of the Term

2.2   Wherever the context so admits the expression 'the Tenant' includes
the person(s) deriving title under him

2.3   Where the Landlord or the Tenant for the time being comprises two
or more persons obligations expressed or implied to be made by or
with them are deemed to be made by or with such persons jointly
and severally

2.4   Words importing one gender include all other genders, words
importing the singular include the plural and vice versa and words
importing persons shall be construed as importing a corporate body
or a partnership and vice versa

2.5   References in this Agreement to any clause, subclause or schedule
without further designation shall be construed as a reference to the
clause, subclause or schedule to this Agreement so numbered

2.6   The clause, paragraph and schedule headings do not form part of this
agreement and shall not be taken into account in its construction or
interpretation

2.7   References to any statute or statutory section shall include any
statutory amendment, modification or re-enactment of it for the time
being in force and shall subordinate legislation made under it

2.8   Any covenant by the Tenant not to do any act or thing shall include
an obligation not to permit or suffer that act or thing to be done

2.9   References to any right of the Landlord to have access to or entry
upon the Property shall be construed as extending [to any superior
landlord] and to all persons authorised by the Landlord [or any
superior landlord]

2.10   References to the Premises include references to any part or parts of
the Premises and to the fixtures, [furnishings, furniture] and contents
as set out in the Inventory

[1.3]

3. Agreement

3.1 The Landlord agrees to let and the Tenant agrees to take the Premises for the Term at the Rent

3.2 This Agreement is intended to create an assured shorthold tenancy under the Housing Act 1988[9]

[3.3 The Premises are let together with the right(s) for the Tenant set out in Schedule 1 and excepting and reserving for the Landlord the rights set out in Schedule 2][10]

[1.4]

4. Tenant's Agreements

The Tenant agrees with the Landlord as follows:

4.1.1 Rent

To pay the Rent to [the Landlord *OR* the Agent] during the Term by equal [weekly *OR* monthly *OR* quarterly] instalments of [£   ] in advance[11] [[by standing order *OR* direct debit] to [*details of account*] (whether formally demanded or not)[12]

4.1.2 Outgoings

To pay all rates, taxes, charges, outgoings, assessments and impositions which are now or during the Term charged assessed or imposed upon the Premises or upon the owner or occupier of them including council tax, or any tax replacing it, provided that the Tenant shall not be responsible for any of the same payable by the Landlord in respect of any disposition of or dealing with his reversionary interest in the Premises [or any rent, service charges or other sums payable by the Landlord under the Headlease[13]]

4.1.3 Services

4.1.3.1 To pay and indemnify the Landlord against:

4.1.3.1.1 All water and sewage charges and metered payments in respect of the supply of water to the Premises

4.1.3.1.2 All charges for gas and electricity consumed on

or supplied to the Premises and the standing charge or charges and any metered rent

4.1.3.1.3   All charges made for the use of telephones on the Premises, including rental and any additional charges for repair, maintenance and reconnection

4.1.3.1.4   The amount of the BBC television licence fee [and of any charges for [cable, Sky or satellite] television services for the Premises]

4.1.3.1.5   All charges for the security alarm or other security system at the Premises together with any and all 'call out' charges resulting from the security alarm or other security systems at the Premises being activated, whether or not intentionally, during the Term[14]

4.1.4   To ensure that all accounts issued by the relevant authorities or suppliers are issued to, and made out to the Tenant for the duration of the Term and to settle all such accounts within a reasonable period of receipt of them. If any service or facility or disconnection for non-payment of an account, to pay the reconnection charges and to indemnify the Landlord against any demands or claims made in respect of them [to ensure that all accounts issued by the relevant authorities or suppliers are re-addressed to the Landlord at the end of the Term]

4.1.5   Repair and Maintenance[15]

4.1.5.1   To keep all parts of the Premises not the responsibility of the Landlord pursuant to Section 11 of the Landlord and Tenant Act 1985 in good and clean repair and condition (fair wear and tear and damage by the risks which are to be insured against by the Landlord excepted unless the relevant policy of insurance is rendered void or voidable, or payment of the whole or part of the insurance monies is refused in consequence of some act or default on the part of, or suffered by, the Tenant)

4.1.5.2   To advise the Landlord immediately of any items of disrepair for which the Landlord is liable

4.1.5.3   Immediately to replace all cracked or broken glass, defective tap washers, electric light bulbs and fuses and to inform the Landlord of any such replacements

4.1.5.4 To clean the windows and the glass in any exterior doors [at least [once in each month] during the Term]

4.1.5.5 Not to do any thing or omit to do any thing that will or may cause destruction to the gutters, sewers, drains, sanitary apparatus, water and waste pipes and ducts exclusively serving or forming part of the Premises and to use reasonable endeavours to prevent such destruction and to take adequate precautions to avoid damage from the freezing and bursting of pipes[16]

4.1.5.6 To use reasonable endeavours to keep the Premises free from pests and vermin and to advise the Landlord immediately of any infestation of insects, vermin, wet or dry rot or of any disrepair which if continued might cause further damage to the Premises or a danger to any person

4.1.5.7 To preserve the [furniture, furnishings,] fixtures and other items more particularly described in the Inventory from being destroyed or damaged and not to remove them from the Premises

4.1.5.8 At the end of the Term to pay for the washing and cleaning of all carpets, curtains, linens, counterpanes, blankets, upholstery and similar articles

4.1.5.9 [To keep the [*garden/terrace/patio etc*] of the Premises clean and tidy and in a proper state of cultivation and not to damage or remove any plants or trees or shrubs]

4.1.6 Decoration and Alterations

4.1.6.1 Not to cut or injure any of the walls or partitions of the Premises nor make any additions whatsoever to the Premises nor make any alterations or improvements in the internal arrangements or in the external appearance of the Premises

4.1.6.2 Not to carry out any redecoration of the Premises or any part thereof [without the prior written consent of the Landlord [such consent not to be unreasonably withheld or delayed]][17]

4.1.6.3 Not to do anything or omit to do anything upon the Premises which shall cause damage to, or deterioration of, its internal or external services or to the coverings or decorations of those surfaces. [Save that the Tenant shall be permitted to hang a reasonable number of pictures provided that they are hung using good quality picture hooks [provided that at the end of the Term the walls are made good to the reasonable satisfaction of the Landlord]]

4.1.6.4   Not to affix or exhibit on or from the Property so as to be visible outside of it, any placard, sign, or poster of any description or any aerial or satellite dish and not to hang or allow to be hung any clothes or other articles at the Premises or from the windows at the Premises

4.1.7   Security and Keys

4.1.7.1   Not to alter or change or install any locks or security codes without the prior written consent of the Landlord and to supply the Landlord with a set of keys or the new codes immediately upon replacement

4.1.7.2   To report immediately to the Landlord if keys or security codes or devices are lost or compromised during the Term and to take immediate steps to provide new keys and/or new security codes or devices, supplying the Landlord with a set of keys or the new code or device immediately upon replacement

4.1.7.3   To hand-over to [the Landlord or the Agent] all keys and security devices or codes by 12 noon on the date that the Term ends

4.1.7.4   When the Premises are left unattended to fasten security securely or deadlocks or other locks fitted to the doors and windows permitting access to the Premises and to ensure that the security alarms or other security devices are set at all appropriate times

4.1.7.5   Not to leave the Premises vacant or unoccupied for a period of in excess of [28] consecutive days without first giving written notice to the [Landlord OR Agent] of the intention to do so

4.1.8   Use of the Premises

4.1.8.1   To use the Premises solely for private residential purposes in the occupation of the Tenant [and the Tenant's immediate family and reasonable visitors] and not to carry on or permit to be carried on upon the Premises any profession, trade or business whatsoever nor allow the Premises to be used for illegal, immoral or improper purposes[18]

4.1.8.2   Not to assign, underlet, charge or part with or share the possession or occupation of the Premises or any part of it nor take in any lodger or paying guest[19]

4.1.8.3   Not to keep or allow to be kept on the Premises any animal, reptile or bird [without the consent in writing of the Landlord which may be withdrawn in the event that the animal, reptile or bird causes damage to the Premises or a nuisance or annoyance to the Landlord or to the owners or occupiers of adjoining premises][20]

4.1.8.4   Not to do any act or thing which may be a nuisance or annoyance to the Landlord or to the owners or occupiers of any adjoining premises or which may vitiate any insurance of the Premises or otherwise increase the ordinary premium payable for it

4.1.8.5   Not to obstruct any access to the Property

4.1.8.6   Not to engage any contractor or otherwise incur expenditure on the Landlord's behalf (except in case of emergency) without the prior written approval of the Landlord or the Agent

4.1.9   Costs

4.1.9.1   To pay to the Landlord all charges, costs and expenses (including for the avoidance of doubt, professional fees) incurred by the Landlord in connection with a breach by the Tenant of any obligation on the part of the Tenant contained in this Agreement

4.1.9.2   To pay to the Landlord all charges, costs and expenses (including professional fees and VAT) of and in connection with all applications by the Tenant for any consent or approval of the Landlord required by the terms of this Agreement, including those incurred in cases where the consent is refused or the application is withdrawn

4.1.9.3   To pay the costs and expenses (including solicitor's costs and surveyor's fees) incurred by the Landlord in connection with any Notice served under Section 146 of the Law of Property Act 1925 requiring the Tenant to remedy a breach of any terms of this Tenancy notwithstanding that forfeiture may be avoided otherwise than by relief granted by the Court

4.1.10 Entry[21]

4.1.10.1 To permit the Landlord, with any necessary contractors and workmen, to enter the Premises at all reasonable times upon [24 hours] prior notice or, in the event of emergency at any time without notice, causing as little inconvenience to the Tenant as reasonably practicable and making good any damage caused to the Premises:

4.1.10.1.1 to examine the state and condition of the Premises;

4.1.10.1.2 to carry out any repairs that are necessary pursuant to the Landlord's responsibilities under this Agreement or by statute;

4.1.10.1.3 to carry out works that may be required to repair, [alter or improve] the Premises or the electrical wiring, gas and water pipes or drains in or under the Premises or any part of it [and to carry out repairs [alterations, improvements, rebuilding or other works] to the Building that can only be carried out by having access to the Premises or the electrical wiring, gas and water pipes or drains within or sharing it];

4.1.10.1.4 to permit the Landlord and all those authorised by him during the last [   ] of the Term (however it ends) or at any time during the Term in the event of the Landlord wishing to sell or otherwise deal with its reversion, to view the Premises

4.1.11 Notice to Repair

To permit the [Landlord *OR* Agent] to give to the Tenant notice in writing of all works of repair, redecoration, cultivation or otherwise which should have been carried out by the Tenant under the terms of this Agreement and, if the Tenant fails to execute the same within [one month] of service of such notice, to permit the Landlord to enter upon the Premises and execute such works at the expense of the

Tenant and to pay to the Landlord the expenses of any such work upon demand on a full indemnity basis

4.1.12 Other Requirements

4.1.12.1 To comply with any requirements from time to time of the Landlord's insurers in respect of any insurance policy for the Premises provide that the Landlord shall notify the Tenant of the same

[4.1.12.2 Not to do anything or omit to do anything that puts the Landlord in breach of its obligations under the Headlease]*[22]*

[4.1.12.3 To observe and perform [*specify the provisions*] of the Headlease]*[23]*

4.1.13 Yielding Up

At the expiration or sooner determination of the tenancy created by this Agreement to deliver up to the Landlord the Property in good and clean repair and condition as required by the terms of this Agreement*[24]*. Not to remove any of the fixtures, [furniture] and household effects (or any articles substituted for them) from the Premises and to leave them at the end of the tenancy created by this Agreement in the several rooms and places as described in the Inventory or as found at the commencement of the Term

[1.5]

5. Landlord's Agreements

The Landlord agrees with the Tenant as follows

5.1 Insurance

To keep the Premises insured [or procure that the Premises are insured] against loss or damage by fire, tempest, flood, burst pipes or explosion and such other risks usually comprised in a Home Owner's comprehensive buildings insurance policy including public liability to any third party, but the Landlord does not agree to insure any fixtures, fittings or contents that are the property of the Tenant

5.2 Quiet Enjoyment

To permit the Tenant to hold the Property peaceably and without any interruption by the Landlord or any person lawfully claiming under or in trust for the Landlord

5.3 Repair

To comply with the Landlord's repairing obligations under Section 11 of the Landlord and Tenant Act 1985

5.4 Delivery

To deliver to the Tenant the Premises at the commencement of the Term in a clean and tidy condition [having been professionally cleaned]

[1.6]

6. Landlord's Declarations

6.1   The Landlord confirms that he has the title and power to enter into this Agreement and that all necessary licences and consents (if any) have been obtained[25]

6.2   The Landlord confirms that all upholstered furniture, soft furnishings, bed mattresses, pillows and cushions supplied to the Premises comply with the provisions of The Furniture and Furnishings (Fire) (Safety) Regulations 1998 and The Furniture and Furnishings (Fire) (Safety) (Amendment) Regulations 1993[26]

6.3   The Landlord confirms that all gas appliances with the Premises comply with the Gas Safety (Installation and Use) Regulations 1998[27] and all electrical equipment within the Premises complies with the Electrical Equipment (Safety) Regulations 1994[28]

6.4   The Landlord confirms that a valid certificate issued by a CORGI registered engineer certifying that all gas appliances to the Property comply with the Gas Safety (Installation and Use) Regulations 1998 is in place throughout the Term

[1.7]

7. Mutual Agreements

7.1 Deposit

7.1.1   The Tenant must pay the Deposit to the [Landlord OR the Agents] [on the first day of the Term] to be held by them as stakeholders, to be applied towards the discharge or part discharge of any liability referred to in this clause

7.1.2   The [Landlord *OR* Agent] may retain from the Deposit [and may pay to the Landlord]:

7.1.2.1   any rent or other payments due from the Tenant to the Landlord, including advance rent that has fallen due;

7.1.2.2   any sum the Landlord expends or incurs in remedying any failure by the Tenant to comply with his obligations under this Agreement; and

7.1.2.3   any interest due under this Agreement on any of the above from the date payment is due to the date it is deducted from the Deposit,

but shall not be obliged to do so

7.1.3   If the Landlord does apply the Deposit or any part of it as authorised above, the Tenant must, at the Landlord's written request, pay the Landlord a further sum to restore the Deposit to the agreed amount

7.1.4   Subject to the provisions of Clause 7.1.2, the Landlord must return the Deposit or the balance of it to the Tenant as soon as possible after the end of the Term [with interest *OR* that any interest earned on the Deposit may be retained by the Landlord]

7.1.5   In no case shall any part of the Deposit be treated as rent or release the Tenant of its obligations to make all payments or Rent, clear of all deductions

7.2 Interest[29]

If any Rent or other money payable by the Tenant to the Landlord or the Agents under the provisions of this Agreement is not paid within fourteen days of the day on which it became due it shall be payable with interest on it at the rate of [4%] per annum above the Base Rate of [*name of Bank*] for the time being in force calculated on a day to day basis from the date upon which it became due down to the date of payment

7.3 Recovery of Possession

If and whenever during the Term:

7.3.1   [The Rent is outstanding for [14] days after becoming due whether formally demanded or not[30] (or if the draftsman wishes to set out the grounds in the Housing Act 1988, Schedule 2, Part I, Ground 8 in detail)[31] [(whether rent payable weekly or fortnightly) at least eight weeks' rent lawfully due from the Tenant is unpaid (or where rent payable monthly) at least two months' rent lawfully due from the Tenant is unpaid (or where rent payable quarterly) one quarter's rent lawfully due from the Tenant is more than three months in arrears (or where rent payable yearly) three months' rent lawfully due from the Tenant is more than three months in arrears]]; or

7.3.2   there is a breach by the Tenant of any obligation or other term of this Agreement; or

7.3.3   the grounds for possession in the Housing Act 1988, Schedule 2, Part I, Grounds [2 or] 8 or any of the grounds in Part II of that Schedule other than Grounds 9 or 16 apply[32]; or

7.3.4   the Tenant becomes bankrupt, has an administration order made in respect of his assets, has a receiver appointed, makes an arrangement for the benefit of his creditors, or has any distress or execution levied on his goods;

then the Landlord may bring a court action[33] to recover possession of the Property, even if any previous right to do so has been waived

7.4   Suspension of Rent

If, and whenever during the Term the Premises or any part of it [or means of access to it] is damaged or destroyed by any risk that the Landlord is obliged to insure against under the Terms of this Agreement, then the Rent (or a fair proportion of it according to the nature and extent of the damage) shall cease to be payable for so long as the Premises or any part of it remains unfit for use, the amount, in case of dispute, to be settled by arbitration (provided that this shall not apply if the relevant insurance policy is rendered void or voidable, or payment of the whole or part of the insurance monies is refused in consequence of some act or default on the part of or suffered by the Tenant)

7.5   Notices

7.5.1   The address of the Landlord stated at the head of this Agreement shall be the address in England or Wales at which notices (including notices in proceedings) may be served on him by the Tenant and this provisions shall be deemed to constitute notice for the purposes of Section 48(1) of the Landlord and Tenant Act 1987

7.5.2   Any notice or other document to be served on either of the parties under the terms of or in connection with this Agreement shall be sufficiently served if it is left or delivered at, or sent by registered post or through the recorded delivery system addressed to:

7.5.2.1   the address of the party to be served specified at the head of this Agreement; or

7.5.2.2   such other address as may from time to time be notified in writing to the other party; or

7.5.2.3   (in the case of any notice which is to be served on the Tenant) the Premises

7.5.3   Any notice or document of the kind referred to in this clause if sent by registered post or through the recorded delivery system addressed to any address referred to in this clause shall be deemed to have been sufficiently served 48 hours after the time of posting (unless returned by the Post Office undelivered)

[1.8]

8. Entire Understanding[34]

This Agreement embodies the entire understanding of the parties relating to the Premises and all matters dealt by this Agreement

[1.9]

9. Representations

The Tenant acknowledges that this Agreement has not been entered into in reliance wholly or partly on any statement or representations made by or on behalf of the Landlord except any such statement or presentation expressly set out in this Agreement

[1.10]

10. Severance Clause[35]

If any term of this Agreement is, in whole or in part, held to be a legal or unenforceable to any extent under any enactment or rule of law, that term or part shall to that extent be deemed not to form part of this Agreement and the enforceability of the remainder of this Agreement shall not be affected

[1.11]

11. Jurisdiction

The Landlord and the Tenant agree that this Agreement shall be exclusively governed by and construed in accordance with the Laws of England and Wales and will submit to the exclusive jurisdiction of the English Courts

[1.12]

12. Contracts (**Rights of Third Parties**) Act 1999

This Agreement shall not operate to confer any rights on any third party and no person other than the parties to it may enforce any provision of this Agreement by virtue of the Contracts (Rights of Third Parties) Act 1999

SIGNED by the Landlord)

SIGNED by the Tenant)

[1.13]

[SCHEDULE 1

The Rights Granted

The Premises are let together with the following rights:-

[   ]]

[1.14]

[SCHEDULE 2

Rights excepted and reserved

The Demised Premises are let subject to the following exceptions and reservations reserved for the benefit of the Landlord's adjoining premises and every part of them:

[   ]]

Notes to Form 1

1. Note that since 28 February 1997 the Housing Act 1988, s 19A as inserted by the Housing Act 1996, s 96(1) provides that all tenancies of residential properties otherwise qualifying, e g for a term of under 21 years at a rent of less than £25,000 a year etc, are considered to be assured shorthold tenancies. Before that date a notice that the tenancy was to be an assured shorthold tenancy had to be served and the tenancy had to be not determinable by the Landlord for at least six months. No prior notice is now required and there is no minimum period requirement. The Landlord cannot however recover possession under the Housing Act 1988, s 21 during the first six months of the term.

    An assured shorthold tenancy can be created for a fixed term or on a periodic, i e monthly, quarterly etc, basis. The form is for a fixed term.

    The *Guidance on unfair terms in tenancy agreements* (OFT 356, November 2001), inter alia, says:

    'Ordinary words should be used as far as possible, and in their normal sense. However, avoiding the use of technical vocabulary cannot guarantee intelligibility by itself. That also requires clarity in the way terms are organised. Sentences should be short, and the text of the contract should be divided into easily understood sub-headings covering recognisably similar issues. Statutory references, elaborate definitions and extensive cross-referencing between terms should be avoided.' (para 19.7)

    'Where a term is ambiguous, a court may be able to find at least one fair meaning in it, and enforce it on that basis, rather than declaring it unfair and void through lack of clarity. However, the Directive makes clear that the "most favourable interpretation" rule is intended to benefit consumers in private disputes, not to give suppliers a defence against regulatory action (see Regulation 7(2)). If ambiguity in a term could disadvantage tenants it may be challenged as unfair, even if one of its possible meanings is fair.' (para 19.6)

    'Fairness is not a matter of rigid prescriptions. The effect of the plain language requirements of the Regulations does not mean that all tenants must understand every word of every contract. Fairness requires that they have a real chance to learn, by the time the contract is binding, about terms that might otherwise disadvantage them. This can be achieved in various ways. Within the contract, significant points can be highlighted and unavoidable technicalities explained. Explanatory material, such as a summary, can also be provided alongside the contract. And information can be conveyed earlier on, in brochures and even advertisements. Preferably, of course, suppliers will use more than one such means.' (para 19.9).

    The Tenant would be wise to ascertain whether the Landlord's title is subject to any charges. If it is, the consent of the mortgagees to this agreement should be obtained. Otherwise, the mortgagees are not bound by the agreement and the tenant's possession could be disturbed by the mortgagees seeking possession or exercising their power of sale.

2. See the *Guidance on unfair terms in tenancy agreements* (OFT 356, November 2001) para 14.1.5.

'Such a warning can strengthen written terms, provided that tenants are genuinely likely to see, understand and act on it. If this is the case, there is less scope for misunderstanding, and thus less likelihood of plausible allegations that oral statements were relied on. However, the warning needs to be sufficiently highlighted in some way in order to draw it to the tenant's attention. Moreover, the agreement must be drafted in plain intelligible language, or the Tenant will be unable to spot a potential contradiction between what is said and what is printed.' (para 14.1.6).

3. Applicable where the Landlord is a company registered outside of England and Wales or an individual who resides out of England and Wales.

4. Applicable where an agent is appointed to collect the rent and/or manage the Premises on behalf of the landlord.

5. Applicable where the Premises forms part of a larger building as in the case of a flat.

6. Applicable where the Landlord is a Tenant under a lease. This will, of course, often be the case where the Premises is a flat.

7. The rent payable under an assured shorthold tenancy or an assured tenancy is as agreed between the Landlord and the Tenant, but it should be noted that if the rent exceeds £25,000 a year it takes the tenancy out of the category of assured tenancies, and therefore assured shorthold tenancies and if the Tenant thinks that the rent is excessive he can refer it to the local rent assessment committee which, if there is a sufficient number of similar lettings and if they are satisfied that the rent charged is significantly higher than the level of rents under such lettings, may determine a rent from such date as it may direct: see the Housing Act 1988, s 22. However, the Tenant may only refer his rent to the committee during the first six months of his period of occupation.

The periods by reference to which rent is payable are of importance if the Tenant holds over at the end of a fixed term tenancy, whether the periodic tenancy that arises is implied by the common law or by statute. Under the common law, the Tenant under a tenancy agreement for one year at a rent of £x a week who holds over becomes a weekly tenant: *Adler v Blackman* [1953] 1 QB 146, [1952] 2 All ER 945, CA. If the fixed term tenancy is an assured tenancy, at the end of the term the Tenant is entitled to remain in possession under a periodic tenancy the periods of which are the same as those for which the rent was last payable under the fixed term tenancy: see the Housing Act 1988, s 5(2),(3).

8. If the term is longer than three years Form 4 should be used. Care must be taken as to the legal consequences if the date stated for commencement of the term is earlier than the date of the lease. For example, in a lease where provisions were to apply if 50 years of the term had expired, the time was reckoned from the date of the lease and not from an earlier date mentioned from which the term was to run: *Earl of Cadogan v Guinness* [1936] Ch 515, [1936] 2 All ER 29; *Colton v Becollda Property Investments Ltd* [1950] 1 KB 216, CA. The habendum of the lease marks the duration of the tenant's interest so the Landlord has no action for breach of covenant committed before the date of the lease: *Shaw v Kay* (1847) 1 Exch 412.

9. Even without this clause, which is put in principally for information, the tenancy will be an assured shorthold Tenant if it qualifies.

10. Careful consideration should be given to rights and reservations. For example, rights relating to access, use of lifts, common areas, communal gardens etc. Reservations may be necessary, for example, to allow a right of way over a garden to access neighbouring land.

11. In the absence of an express provision rent is payable in arrears.
12. Provisions excluding the right of 'set off' are common. The *Guidance on unfair terms in tenancy agreements* (OFT 356, November 2001) says:

    'Terms which limit or deprive the consumer of access to redress, as well as those which disclaim liability may be considered unfair. One legitimate way for a consumer to obtain compensation from a supplier is to exercise the right to set-off. Where a consumer has an arguable claim under the contract against a supplier, the law generally allows the amount of that claim to be deducted from anything the consumer has to pay. This helps prevent unnecessary legal proceedings'. (para 2.5.1)

    'If the right of set-off is excluded, tenants may have (or believe they have) no choice but to pay their rent in full, even where they have incurred costs as a result of a breach of an obligation by the landlord. To obtain redress, they then have to go to court. The costs, delays and uncertainties involved may, in practice force them to give up their claim, and deprive them of their rights. The right of set-off should be exercised by tenants only with caution and preferably on legal advice. However, that does not justify terms which stop them from exercising it at all. The OFT does not object to terms that deter tenants from using the right of set-off to withhold excessively large sums.' (paras 2.5.2, 2.5.3)

13. Applicable where the Landlord is a Tenant under a long lease that reserves ground rent, service charge etc.
14. A term that requires the Tenant always to meet charges that could arise through the Landlord's default in carrying out repairing obligations is open to objection see the *Guidance on unfair terms in tenancy agreements* (OFT 356, November 2001) para 2.3.2.
15. Ensure that the repairing obligations of the parties complement each other and suit the type of property and length of term. Where the tenancy is for a short term the Tenant is usually made responsible for the interior, so far a permitted by statue.
16. Regard must be had to the provisions of the Landlord and Tenant Act 1985, ss 11–15.
17. It is usual in a short term tenancy to prohibit alterations or additions to the dwelling and any garden or grounds absolutely.
18. The clause should not be unreasonably restrictive. The *Guidance on unfair terms in tenancy agreements* (OFT 356, November 2001) says:

    'Terms that ban overnight guests may be seen as producing an unnecessary and unreasonable restriction on normal and harmless use and enjoyment of the property. This term could also cause hardship and suffering, for example, if a tenant's daytime visitor falls ill'. (para 18.8.7, 7th example)

19. It is a term of every assured periodic tenancy that, except with the consent of the landlord, the Tenant must not: (1) assign the tenancy in whole or in part; or (2) sublet or part with possession of the whole or any part of the dwelling house let on the tenancy: see the Housing Act 1988, s 15(1). The Landlord and Tenant Act 1927, s 19 (consent to assign not to be unreasonably withheld etc) is specifically excluded in the case of such implied terms (see the Housing Act 1988, s 15(2)), and the Landlord may, therefore, refuse consent arbitrarily. It is not, therefore, necessary to include an express prohibition in an agreement for a periodic tenancy that is and always will be an assured tenancy. If an absolute prohibition is required in an

assured tenancy this may be included as an express covenant, as permitted by the Housing Act 1988, s 15(3)(a). In the case of a short fixed term an absolute prohibition on dealings is usual.

20. In relation to a total ban on keeping pets, the *Guidance on unfair terms in tenancy agreements* (OFT 356, November 2001) says:

> 'Such a term has been considered unfair under comparable legislation in another EU state because it could prevent a Tenant keeping a goldfish. A term prohibiting the keeping of pets that could harm the property or be a nuisance to other residents would be unlikely to meet the same objection.' (para 18.8.5, 8th example)

21. The agreement should be tailored to ensure that the Landlord has access to fulfil all his obligations as well as to check on the state of the Premises, but rights of entry must not be excessive. The *Guidance on unfair terms in tenancy agreements* (OFT 356, November 2001) says:

> 'A term dealing with rights of entry is unlikely to be challenged if it reflects the ordinary legal position. This recognises that a Landlord who is responsible for carrying out repairs to the property needs reasonable access for two specific purposes: firstly, in order to check whether repairs are necessary, and secondly, to carry them out. Reasonable access means access at reasonable times, and with reasonable notice, except in cases of urgency.' (para 2.7.5)

22. Applicable as with 6 above. It is advisable given the provisions of the *Guidance of unfair terms in tenancy agreements* (OFT 356, November 2001) that the Tenant is given a copy of any Headlease together with an explanation of the terms if they are at all unclear.

23. Care must be taken to ensure that a Landlord who is a Tenant under a Headlease highlights particular covenants continued in that Lease. This may be the case in the care of Regulations that apply to the Building.

24. The agreement should be tailored to suit the tenant's repairing obligations.

25. For example, consents required under the terms of the Landlord's mortgage or a Landlord's consent required by the terms of the Headlease.

26. The Furniture and Furnishings (Fire) (Safety) Regulations 1988, SI 1988/1324 as amended by SI 1993/207 provide that where furniture or furnishings are supplied 'in the course of business' (but even domestic owners who have never granted a tenancy before are likely to be doing so 'as a business' unless the letting is to a family member) must ensure that such furniture etc complies with the regulations as to fire retardant materials. The covers and the fillings or anything upholstered or which has filling material e g beds, mattresses, headboards, sofas and chairs fitted with loose covers, futons, cushions and pillows, garden furniture and nursery furniture are within the regulations. Items manufactured before 1950, together with carpets, curtains, duvets and loose covers for mattresses are outside the regulations. Compliance can be proved by manufacturers labels, receipts for purchase or certificates by interior designers. Failure to comply can result in prosecution by the Trading Standards Office and conviction can result in a fine of up to £5,000 or six months' imprisonment.

27. The Gas Safety (Installation and Use) Regulations 1998, SI 1998/2451 relate to gas appliances in all let residential properties. All appliances must be tested by a CORGI registered engineer. A Landlord's safety certificate must be provided to the Tenant upon occupation or within 28 days of a certificate or renewal certificate

being issued. It is advised that landlords should have additional checks carried out between tenancies. Failure to comply is a criminal offence enforced by Health and Safety Executive and conviction will result in a fine of up to £5,000 or six months' imprisonment.

28. The Electrical Equipment (Safety) Regulations 1994, SI 1994/3260 provides that all electrical appliances and equipment must be tested and a portable appliance test certificate obtained, but there is no provision as to when this has to be done. New electrical appliances usually have a statement as to testing. It is advised that the Landlord should have all appliances tested where it is not evident that this has been done, or re-tested, before the grant of any tenancy agreement. Non-compliance could mean prosecution by the Trading Standards Office and results in a fine of up to £5,000 or six months' imprisonment.

29. The rate of interest should be fair. The *Guidance of unfair terms in tenancy agreements* (OFT 356, November 2001) says:

> 'A requirement to pay unreasonable interest on arrears of rent, for instance at a rate substantially above the clearing banks' base rates, is likely to be regarded as an unfair penalty. The Tenant would have to pay more than the cost of making up the deficit caused by the tenant's default. A Landlord's personal circumstances may expose him to an interest rate which would normally be considered excessive when passed on to a tenant. In this case, it may not be unfair to require tenants who default on their rent to pay a similar high rate on their arrears provided the reason for this was explained and drawn to their attention at the time of entering into the agreement.' (para 5.2)

30. In the absence of these words a formal demand must be served.

31. It may be thought necessary in view of the requirements that forfeiture clauses should acknowledge the tenant's legal rights and be intelligible to the ordinary person: see the *Guidance on unfair terms in tenancy agreements* (OFT 356, November 2001) para 18.3.3. A clause giving the impression that a Tenant can be evicted if the rent is in arrear for less than the period required under the Housing Act would seem to be in grave danger of being found unfair.

32. The court may not make an order for possession of a dwelling house let on a fixed term assured shorthold tenancy during the fixed term unless: (1) the ground for possession is Ground 2 or 8 or one of Grounds 10–15 inclusive in the Housing Act 1988, Sch 2; and (2) the terms of the tenancy make provision for it to be brought to an end on the ground in question, whether in the form of a provision for re-entry, for forfeiture, for determination by notice or otherwise: see the Housing Act 1988, s 7(6). As in the case of rent arrears, setting out the provisions in full may be advisable.

33. The *Guidance of unfair terms in tenancy agreements* (OFT 356, November 2001) says:

> 'Forfeiture or re-entry clauses need to acknowledge the tenant's legal rights, at least in general terms, to be more acceptable. They also need to be intelligible to an ordinary person. Terms which do not make it clear that it is unlawful for a Landlord to evict a Tenant and re-enter the property without a court order may be open to objection. Although, it may be helpful to advise the Tenant to seek independent legal advice where eviction is threatened, this will not be enough to avoid unfairness if the term does not clearly refer to the need for court proceedings.' (para 18.3.3)

34. The *Guidance on unfair terms in tenancy agreements* (OFT 356, November 2001) says

> 'It is central to good faith in any agreement that the parties will keep their word. Good faith demands not only that the parties to a contract are bound by their promises, but also by any other statements they or their representatives make to secure the other person's agreement. If a standard term excludes liability for these unwritten promises and statements, there is considerable scope for prospective tenants to be misled about their rights when the Landlord fails to comply with any obligations or understandings.' (para 14.1.1)

35. Any unfair term does not bind the tenant, but the remainder of the tenancy continues in force if it is capable of continuing in existence without the unfair term: see the Unfair Terms in Consumer Contracts Regulations 1999, SI 1999/2083, reg 8(1),(2).

Form 2
Agreement for a fixed term (of three years or less) that is not assured suitable for house or flat[1]

TAKE NOTICE THAT THIS TENANCY AGREEMENT IS A BINDING DOCUMENT. BEFORE SIGNING IT YOU SHOULD READ IT CARE-FULLY TO ENSURE THAT IT CONTAINS EVERYTHING YOU DO WANT AND NOTHING THAT IS UNACCEPTABLE TO YOU[2]

THIS AGREEMENT is made the   day of
[   ]

BETWEEN
(1) [   ] [company Registration Number] [of
     [   ] *OR* whose registered office is at
     [   ]] ('the Landlord') [and whose address for service
     in England and Wales is at [   ][3]]
(2) [   ] of [   ] ('the Tenant')

[2.1]

1. Definitions

'**the Agent**' means [   ] of [   ][4]

['**the Building**' means the building known as [   ] of which
     the Premises form part[5]]

'**the Deposit**' means the sum of £[   ]

['**the Headlease**' means the lease dated   ] and made
     between [   ] (1) and [   ] (2)][6]

'**the Inventory**' means the list of [furniture, furnishings] fixtures and other
     items in the Premises which will be signed by both parties prior to
     commencement of the Term and which records their present state
     and condition

'**the Premises**' means [[the flat numbered [   ] on the
     [   ] floor at the Building] *OR* [the house known
     as [   ]] [shown for identification purposes only
     edged [red] on the plan annexed to this Agreement]

'**the Rent**' means £[   ] a [year *OR* month *OR* week][7]

'**the Term**' [   ] from and including [   ]
and any period of holding over or extension or continuance by
statute or common law[8]

[2.2]

2. Interpretation

2.1   Wherever the context so admits the expression 'the Landlord'
includes the person for the time being entitled to the reversion
immediately expectant on the determination of the Term

2.2   Wherever the context so admits the expression 'the Tenant' includes
the person(s) deriving title under him

2.3   Where the Landlord or the Tenant for the time being comprises two
or more persons obligations expressed or implied to be made by or
with them are deemed to be made by or with such persons jointly
and severally

2.4   Words importing one gender include all other genders and words
importing the singular include the plural and vice versa and words
importing persons shall be construed as importing a corporate body
or a partnership and vice versa

2.5   References in this Agreement to any clause, subclause or schedule
without further designation shall be construed as a reference to the
clause, subclause or schedule to this Agreement so numbered

2.6   The clause, paragraph and schedule headings do not form part of this
agreement and shall not be taken into account in its construction or
interpretation

2.7   References to any statute or statutory section shall include any
statutory amendment, modification or re-enactment of it for the time
being in force and shall subordinate legislation made under it

2.8   Any covenant by the Tenant not to do any act or thing shall include
an obligation not to permit or suffer that act or thing to be done

2.9   References to any right of the Landlord to have access to or entry
upon the Property shall be construed as extending [to any superior
landlord] and to all persons authorised by the Landlord [or any
superior landlord]

2.10   References to the Premises include references to any part or parts of
the Premises and to the fixtures, [furnishings, furniture] and contents
as set out in the Inventory

[2.3]

3. Agreement

3.1   The Landlord agrees to let and the Tenant agrees to take the Premises for the Term at the Rent

[RESIDENT LANDLORD][9A]

3.2   It is agreed and declared that:

the Premises forms part only at a [building that is not a purpose–built block of flats OR flat that forms part of a purpose–built block of flats] see the Housing Act 1988, s 1, Schedule 1, Part III, Paragraph 22;

the Landlord occupies as his only or principal home another dwellinghouse that also forms part at the [building OR flat] within the meaning of the Housing Act 1988, Schedule 1 paragraph 10; and

the Tenant was not, alone or jointly with others, immediately before the grant of this tenancy a tenant under an assured tenancy within the meaning of the Housing Act 1988, granted by the Landlord, at the Premises or at another dwellinghouse forming part of the building of which the Premises forms part;

the Tenant acknowledges that the tenancy created by this Agreement is not an assured tenancy by reason of the tenancy being granted by a resident landlord [as stated above.]

[TENANCY AT A HIGH RENT][9B]

3.2   The Tenant acknowledges that the tenancy created by this Agreement is not an assured tenancy within the meaning of the Housing Act 1988 by reason of it being a tenancy under which the rent payable for the time being is payable at a rate exceeding £25,000 per annum within the meaning of the Housing Act 1988, Schedule 1, Paragraph 2.]

[LOW RENT][9C]

3.2   The Tenant acknowledges that the tenancy created by this Agreement is not an assured tenancy within the meaning of the Housing Act 1988 by reason of being a tenancy [under which for the time being no rent is payable OR under which the rent payable for the time being is payable at a rate of [£1,000 or less a year, the Premises being in Greater London *OR* £250 or less a year, the Premises being outside Greater London]] within the meaning of the Housing Act 1988 Schedule 1 Paragraph 3.]

[COMPANY][9D]

The Tenant acknowledges that the tenancy created by this Agreement is not an assured tenancy within the meaning of the Housing Act 1988 by reason of the Tenant being a company and not an individual.]

[3.3   The Premises are let together with the right(s) for the Tenant set out in Schedule 1 and excepting and reserving for the Landlord the rights set out in Schedule 2][10]

[2.4]

4. Tenant's agreements

The Tenant agrees with the Landlord as follows:

4.1.1 Rent

To pay the Rent to [the Landlord *OR* the Agent] during the Term by equal [weekly *OR* monthly *OR* quarterly] instalments of [£   ] in advance[11] [[by standing order *OR* direct debit] to [*details of account*] (whether formally demanded or not)[12]

4.1.2 Outgoings

To pay all rates taxes charges outgoings assessments and impositions which are now or during the Term charged assessed or imposed upon the Premises or upon the owner or occupier of them including council tax, or any tax replacing it, provided that the Tenant shall not be responsible for any of the same payable by the Landlord in respect of any disposition of or dealing with his reversionary interest in the Premises [or any rent, service charges or other sums payable by the Landlord under the Headlease[13]]

4.1.3 Services

4.1.3.1   To pay and indemnify the Landlord against:
4.1.3.1.1   All water and sewage charges and metered payments in respect of the supply of water to the Premises

4.1.3.1.2   All charges for gas and electricity consumed on or supplied to the Premises and the standing charge or charges and any metered rent

4.1.3.1.3   All charges made for the use of telephones on the Premises, including rental and any additional charges for repair, maintenance and reconnection

4.1.3.1.4   The amount of the BBC television licence fee [and of any charges for [cable, Sky or satellite] television services for the Premises]

4.1.3.1.5   All charges for the security alarm or other security system at the Premises together with any and all 'call out' charges resulting from the security alarm or other security systems at the Premises being activated during the Term[14]

4.1.4   To ensure that all accounts issued by the relevant authorities or suppliers are issued to and made out to the Tenant for the duration of the Term and to settle all such accounts within a reasonable period of receipt of them. If any service or facility or disconnection for non-payment of an account, to pay the reconnection charges and to indemnify the Landlord against any demands or claims made in respect of them [to ensure that all accounts issued by the relevant authorities or suppliers are re-addressed to the Landlord at the end of the Term]

4.1.5   Repair and maintenance[15]

4.1.5.1   To keep all parts of the Premises not the responsibility of the Landlord pursuant to Section 11 of the Landlord and Tenant Act 1985 in good and clean repair and condition (fair wear and tear and damage by the risks which are to be insured against by the Landlord excepted unless the relevant policy of insurance is rendered void or voidable, or payment of the whole or part of the insurance monies is refused in consequence of some act or default on the part of, or suffered by, the Tenant)

4.1.5.2   To advise the Landlord immediately of any items of disrepair for which the Landlord is liable

4.1.5.3   Immediately to replace all cracked or broken glass, defective tap washers, electric light bulbs and fuses and to inform the Landlord of any such replacements

4.1.5.4   To clean the windows and the glass in any exterior doors [at least [once in each month] during the Term]

4.1.5.5   Not to do any thing or omit to do any thing that will may or cause destruction to the gutters, sewers, drains, sanitary apparatus, water and waste pipes and ducts exclusively serving or forming part of the Premises and to use reasonable endeavours to prevent such destruction and to take adequate precautions to avoid damage from the freezing and bursting of pipes*[16]*

4.1.5.6   To use reasonable endeavours to keep the Premises free from pests and vermin and to advise the Landlord immediately of any infestation of insects, vermin, wet or dry rot or of any disrepair which if continued might cause further damage to the Premises or a danger to any person

4.1.5.7   To preserve the [furniture, furnishings,] fixtures and other items more particularly described in the Inventory from being destroyed or damaged and not to remove them from the Premises

4.1.5.8   At the end of the Term to pay for the washing and cleaning of all carpets, curtains, linens, counterpanes, blankets, upholstery and similar articles

4.1.5.9   [To keep the [*garden/terrace/patio etc*] of the Premises clean and tidy and in a proper state of cultivation and not to damage or remove any plants or trees or shrubs]

4.1.6   Decoration and alterations

4.1.6.1   Not to cut or injure any of the walls or partitions of the Premises nor make any additions whatsoever to the Premises nor make any alterations or improvements in the internal arrangements or in the external appearance of the Premises

4.1.6.2   Not to carry out any redecoration of the Premises or any part thereof [without the prior written consent of the Landlord [such consent not to be unreasonably withheld or delayed]]*[17]*

4.1.6.3   Not to do anything or omit to do anything upon the Premises which shall cause damage to, or deterioration of, its internal or external services or to the coverings or decorations of those surfaces. [Save that the Tenant shall be permitted to hang a reasonable number of pictures provided that they are hung using good quality picture hooks [provided that at the end of the Term the walls are made good to the reasonable satisfaction of the Landlord]]

4.1.6.4 Not to affix or exhibit on or from the Property so as to be visible outside of it, any placard, sign, or poster of any description or any aerial or satellite dish and not to hang or allow to be hung any clothes or other articles at the Premises or from the windows at the Premises

4.1.7 Security and keys

4.1.7.1 Not to alter or change or install any locks or security codes without the prior written consent of the Landlord and to supply the Landlord with a set of keys or the new codes immediately upon replacement

4.1.7.2 To report immediately to the Landlord if keys or security codes or devices are lost or compromised during the Term and to take immediate steps to provide new keys and/or new security codes or devices, supplying the Landlord with a set of keys or the new code or device immediately upon replacement

4.1.7.3 To hand-over to [the Landlord or the Agent] all keys and security devices or codes by 12 noon on the date that the Term ends

4.1.7.4 When the Premises are left unattended to fasten security securely or deadlocks or other locks fitted to the doors and windows permitting access to the Premises and to ensure that the security alarms or other security devices are set at all appropriate times

4.1.7.5 Not to leave the Premises vacant or unoccupied for a period of in excess of [28] consecutive days without first giving written notice to the [Landlord OR Agent] of the intention to do so

4.1.8 Use of the premises

4.1.8.1 To use the Premises solely for private residential purposes in the occupation of the Tenant [and the Tenant's immediate family and reasonable visitors] and not to carry on or permit to be carried on upon the Premises any profession, trade or business whatsoever nor allow the Premises to be used for illegal, immoral or improper purposes[18]

4.1.8.2   Not to assign, underlet, charge or part with or share the possession or occupation of the Premises or any part of it nor take in any lodger or paying guest[19]

4.1.8.3   Not to keep or allow to be kept on the Premises any animal, reptile or bird [without the consent in writing of the Landlord which may be withdrawn in the event that the animal, reptile or bird causes damage to the Premises or a nuisance or annoyance to the Landlord or to the owners or occupiers of adjoining premises][20]

4.1.8.4   Not to any act or thing which may be a nuisance or annoyance to the Landlord or to the owners or occupiers of any adjoining premises or which may vitiate any insurance of the Premises or otherwise increase the ordinary premium payable for it

4.1.8.5   Not to obstruct any access to the Property

4.1.8.6   Not to engage any contractor or otherwise incur expenditure on the Landlord's behalf (except in case of emergency) without the prior written approval of the Landlord or the Agent

4.1.9   Costs

4.1.9.1   To pay to the Landlord all charges, costs and expenses (including for the avoidance of doubt, professional fees) incurred by the Landlord in connection with a breach by the Tenant of any obligation on the part of the Tenant contained in this Agreement

4.1.9.2   To pay to the Landlord all charges, costs and expenses (including professional fees and VAT) of and in connection with all applications by the Tenant for any consent or approval of the Landlord required by the terms of this Agreement, including those incurred in cases where the consent is refused or the application is withdrawn

4.1.9.3   To pay the costs and expenses (including solicitor's costs and surveyor's fees) incurred by the Landlord in connection with any Notice served under Section 146 of the Law of Property Act 1925 requiring the Tenant to remedy a breach of any terms of this Tenancy notwithstanding that forfeiture may be avoided otherwise than by relief granted by the Court

4.1.10 Entry[21]

4.1.10.1 To permit the Landlord, with any necessary contractors and workmen, to enter the Premises at all reasonable times upon [24 hours] prior notice or, in the event of emergency at any time without notice, causing as little inconvenience to the Tenant as reasonably practicable and making good any damage caused to the Premises:

4.1.10.1.1 to examine the state and condition of the Premises;

4.1.10.1.2 to carry out any repairs that are necessary pursuant to the Landlord's responsibilities under this Agreement or by statute;

4.1.10.1.3 to carry out works that may be required to repair, [alter or improve] the Premises or the electrical wiring, gas and water pipes or drains in or under the Premises or any part of it [and to carry out repairs [alterations, improvements, rebuilding or other works] to the Building that can only be carried out by having access to the Premises or the electrical wiring, gas and water pipes or drains within or sharing it]

4.1.10.1.4 to permit the Landlord and all those authorised by him during the last [   ] of the Term (however it ends) or at any time during the Term in the event of the Landlord wishing to sell or otherwise deal with its reversion, to view the Premises

4.1.11 Notice to repair

To permit the [Landlord *OR* the Agent] to give to the Tenant notice in writing of all works of repair, redecoration, cultivation or otherwise which should have been carried out by the Tenant under the terms of this Agreement and, if the Tenant fails to execute the same within [one month] of service of such notice, to permit the Landlord to enter upon the Premises and execute such works at the expense of the

Tenant and to pay to the Landlord the expenses of any such work upon demand on a full indemnity basis

4.1.12 Other requirements

4.1.12.1 To comply with any requirements from time to time of the Landlord's insurers in respect of any insurance policy for the Premises provide that the Landlord shall notify the Tenant of the same

[4.1.12.2 Not to do anything or omit to do anything that puts the Landlord in breach of its obligations under the Headlease][22]

[4.1.12.3 To observe and perform [*specify the provisions*] of the Headlease][23]

4.1.13 Yielding up

At the expiration or sooner determination of the tenancy created by this Agreement to deliver up to the Landlord the Property in good and clean repair and condition as required by the terms of this Agreement[24]. Not to remove any of the fixtures [,furniture] and household effects (or any articles substituted for them) from the Premises and to leave them at the end of the tenancy created by this Agreement in the several rooms and places as described in the Inventory or as found at the commencement of the Term

[2.5]

5. Landlord's Agreements

The Landlord agrees with the Tenant as follows:

5.1 Insurance

To keep the Premises insured [or procure that the Premises are insured] against loss or damage by fire, tempest, flood, burst pipes or explosion and such other risks usually comprised in a Home Owner's comprehensive buildings insurance policy including public liability to any third party, but the Landlord does not agree to insure any fixtures, fittings or contents that are the property of the Tenant

5.2 Quiet enjoyment

To permit the Tenant to hold the Property peaceably and without any interruption by the Landlord or any person lawfully claiming under or in trust for the Landlord

5.3   Repair

To comply with the Landlord's repairing obligations under Section 11 of the Landlord & Tenant Act 1985

5.4   Delivery

To deliver to the Tenant the Premises at the commencement of the Term in a clean and tidy condition [having been professionally cleaned]

[2.6]

6.   Landlord's Declarations

6.1   The Landlord confirms that he has the title and power to enter into this Agreement and that all necessary licences and consents (if any) have been obtained[25]

6.2   The Landlord confirms that all upholstered furniture, soft furnishings, bed mattresses, pillows and cushions supplied to the Premises comply with the provisions of The Furniture and Furnishings (Fire) (Safety) Regulations 1998 and The Furniture and Furnishings (Fire) (Safety) Amendment Regulations 1993[26]

6.3   The Landlord confirms that all gas appliances with the Premises comply with the Gas Safety (Installation and Use) Regulations 1998[27] and all electrical equipment within the Premises complies with the Electrical Equipment (Safety) Regulations 1994[28]

6.4   The Landlord confirms that a valid certificate issued by a CORGI registered engineer certifying that all gas appliances to the Property comply with the Gas Safety (Installation and Use) Regulations 1998 is in place throughout the Term

[2.7]

7.   Mutual Agreements

7.1   Deposit

7.1.1   The Tenant must pay the Deposit to the [Landlord *OR* the Agents] [on the first day of the Term] to be held by them as stakeholders, to be applied towards the discharge or part discharge of any liability referred to in this clause

7.1.2   The [Landlord *OR* Agent] may retain from the Deposit [and may pay to the Landlord]:

7.1.2.1   any rent or other payments due from the Tenant to the Landlord, including advance rent that has fallen due;

7.1.2.2   any sum the Landlord expends or incurs in remedying any failure by the Tenant to comply with his obligations under this Agreement; and

7.1.2.3   any interest due under this Agreement on any of the above from the date payment is due to the date it is deducted from the Deposit,

but shall not be obliged to do so

7.1.3   If the Landlord does apply the Deposit or any part of it as authorised above, the Tenant must, at the Landlord's written request, pay the Landlord a further sum to restore the Deposit to the agreed amount

7.1.4   Subject to the provisions of Clause 7.1.2, the Landlord must return the Deposit or the balance of it to the Tenant as soon as possible after the end of the Term [with interest *OR* that any interest earned on the Deposit may be retained by the Landlord]

7.1.5   In no case shall any part of the Deposit be treated as rent or release the Tenant of its obligations to make all payments or Rent, clear of all deductions

7.2   Interest[29]

If any Rent or other money payable by the Tenant to the Landlord or the Agents under the provisions of this Agreement is not paid within fourteen days or the day on which it became due it shall be payable with interest on it at the rate of [4%] per annum above the Base Rate of [*name of Bank*] for the time being in force calculated on a day to day basis from the date upon which it became due down to the date of payment

7.3   Recovery of possession[30]

7.3.1   The Landlord's rights under this clause arise if and whenever during the Term:

7.3.1.1   the Rent, or any part of it, or any other sum reserved as rent by this lease, lawfully due from the Tenant is unpaid [14 days] after becoming due, whether formally demanded or not[31]; or

7.3.1.2   the Tenant breaches any covenant, condition or other term of this Agreement; or

7.3.1.3   the Tenant, or any person comprised in the Tenant, being an individual, becomes bankrupt or has an interim receiver appointed in respect of his property; or

7.3.1.4   the Tenant, being a company, enters into liquidation whether compulsory or voluntary, but not if the liquidation is for amalgamation or reconstruction of a solvent company, or has a receiver appointed[32]; or

7.3.1.5   the Tenant or any person, comprised in the Tenant enters into an arrangement for the benefit of his creditors; or

7.3.1.6   the Tenant or any person comprised in the Tenant has any distress or execution levied on his goods][33]

even if any previous right of re-entry has been waived

7.3.2   If and whenever during the Term any of the events set out in Clause 7.3.1 occurs, the Landlord may bring an action to recover possession from the Tenant and re-enter the Premises subject:

7.3.2.1   in the case of unpaid rent to the Tenant's right to relief on payment of the arrears and costs, and

7.3.2.2   in the case of a breach of any obligation other than to pay rent, to his obligations to serve notice on the Tenant specifying the breach complained of, requiring its remedy if it is capable of remedy, and requiring the Tenant to pay compensation in any case, and to allow the Tenant a reasonable time to remedy a breach that is capable of remedy

On the making of a court order for possession this tenancy shall cease absolutely, but without prejudice to any rights or remedies that may have accrued to the Landlord against the Tenant, or to the Tenant against the Landlord in respect of any breach of covenant or other term of this Agreement, including the breach in respect of which the re-entry is made

7.4 Suspension of rent

If, and whenever during the Term the Premises or any part of it [or means of access to it] is damaged or destroyed by any risk that the Landlord is obliged to insure against under the Terms of this Agreement, then the Rent (or a fair proportion of it according to the nature and extent of the damage) shall cease to be payable for so long as the Premises or any part of it remains unfit for use, the amount, in case of dispute, to be settled by arbitration (provided that this shall not apply if the relevant insurance policy is rendered void or voidable, or payment of the whole or part of the insurance monies is refused in consequence of some act or default on the part of or suffered by the Tenant)

7.5 Notices

7.5.1   The address of the Landlord stated at the head of this Agreement shall be the address in England or Wales at which notices (including notices in proceedings) may be served on him by the Tenant and this provisions shall be deemed to constitute notice for the purposes of Section 48(1) of the Landlord and Tenant Act 1987

7.5.2   Any notice or other document to be served on either of the parties under the terms of or in connection with this Agreement shall be sufficiently served if it is left or delivered at, or sent by registered post or through the recorded delivery system addressed to:

7.5.2.1   the address of the party to be served specified at the head of this Agreement; or

7.5.2.2   such other address as may from time to time be notified in writing to the other party; or

7.5.2.3   (in the case of any notice which is to be served on the Tenant) the Premises

7.5.3   Any notice or document of the kind referred to in this clause if sent by registered post or through the recorded delivery system addressed to any address referred to in this clause shall be deemed to have been sufficiently served 48 hours after the time of posting (unless returned by the Post Office undelivered)

[2.8]

8. Entire Understanding[34]

This Agreement embodies the entire understanding of the parties relating to the Premises and all matters dealt by this Agreement

[2.9]

9. Representations

The Tenant acknowledges that this Agreement has not been entered into in reliance wholly or partly on any statement or representations made by or on behalf of the Landlord except any such statement or presentation expressly set out in this Agreement

[2.10]

10. Severance Clause[35]

If any term of this Agreement is, in whole or in part, held to be a legal or unenforceable to any extent under any enactment or rule of law, that term or part shall to that extent be deemed not to form part of this Agreement and the enforceability of the remainder of this Agreement shall not be affected

[2.11]

11. Jurisdiction

The Landlord and the Tenant agree that this Agreement shall be exclusively governed by and construed in accordance with the Laws of England and Wales and will submit to the exclusive jurisdiction of the English Courts

[2.12]

12. Contracts (Rights of Third Parties) Act 1999

This Agreement shall not operate to confer any rights on any third party and no person other than the parties to it may enforce any provision of this Agreement by virtue of the Contracts (Rights of Third Parties) Act 1999

SIGNED by the Landlord)

SIGNED by the Tenant)

[2.13]

[SCHEDULE 1

The rights granted

The Premises are let together with the following rights:

[   ]]

[2.14]

[SCHEDULE 2

RIGHTS EXCEPTED AND RESERVED

The Demised Premises are let subject to the following exceptions and reservations reserved for the benefit of the Landlord's adjoining premises and every part of them:

[   ]]

NOTE: Where the Tenant is a company, the following clauses are suggested to replace Clauses 4.1.8.1 and 4.1.8.2 in Form 2.

4.1.8.1 To use the Premises solely for private residential purposes in the occupation of [*name*, [his *OR* her [husband *OR* partner] and [his *OR* her *OR* their] immediate family and staff (if any) [the said *name* being an officer or employee of the Tenant [or such other officer or employee as advised in writing to the [Landlord *OR* Agent]] ('the Occupier') [but the Occupier may only occupy the Premises for as long as he (or she) remains an officer or employee of the Tenant].

4.8.1.2 Subject to the provisions of Clause 4.1.8.1, not to assign, underlet, charge or part with or share the occupation or possession of the Premises or part of it nor take in any lodger or paying guest or to grant or permit to arise any tenancy or other legal interest of the Premises or any part of it in favour of the Occupier, nor permit the Occupier to pay any Rent or make any similar payment.

Notes to Form 2

1. Note that since 28 February 1997 the Housing Act 1988, s 19A as inserted by the Housing Act 1996, s 96(1) provides that all tenancies of residential properties otherwise qualifying, e g for a term of under 21 years at a rent of less than £25,000 a year etc, are considered to be assured shorthold tenancies. Before that date a notice that the tenancy was to be an assured shorthold tenancy had to be served and the tenancy had to be not determinable by the Landlord for at least six months. No prior notice is now required and there is no minimum period requirement.

An assured shorthold tenancy can be created for a fixed term or on a periodic, i e monthly, quarterly etc, basis. The form is for a fixed term.

The *Guidance on unfair terms in tenancy agreements* (OFT 356, November 2001) *inter alia* says:

'Ordinary words should be used as far as possible, and in their normal sense. However, avoiding the use of technical vocabulary cannot guarantee intelligibility by itself. That also requires clarity in the way terms are organised. Sentences should be short, and the text of the contract should be divided into easily understood sub-headings covering recognisably similar issues. Statutory references, elaborate definitions and extensive cross-referencing between terms should be avoided.' (para 19.7)

'Where a term is ambiguous, a court may be able to find at least one fair meaning in it, and enforce it on that basis, rather than declaring it unfair and void through lack of clarity. However, the Directive makes clear that the 'most favourable interpretation' rule is intended to benefit consumers in private disputes, not to give suppliers a defence against regulatory action (see Regulation 7(2)). If ambiguity in a term could disadvantage tenants it may be challenged as unfair, even if one of its possible meanings is fair.' (para 19.6)

'Fairness is not a matter of rigid prescriptions. The effect of the plain language requirements of the Regulations does not mean that all tenants must understand every word of every contract. Fairness requires that they have a real chance to learn, by the time the contract is binding, about terms that might otherwise disadvantage them. This can be achieved in various ways. Within the contract, significant points can be highlighted and unavoidable technicalities explained. Explanatory material, such as a summary, can also be provided alongside the contract. And information can be conveyed earlier on, in brochures and even advertisements. Preferably, of course, suppliers will use more than one such means.' (para 19.9)

The Tenant would be wise to ascertain whether the Landlord's title is subject to any charges. If it is, the consent of the mortgagees to this agreement should be obtained. Otherwise, the mortgagees are not bound by the agreement and the tenant's possession could be disturbed by the mortgagees seeking possession or exercising their power of sale.

2. See the *Guidance on unfair terms in tenancy agreements* (OFT 356, November 2001) para 14.1.5:

'Such a warning can strengthen written terms, provided that tenants are genuinely likely to see, understand and act on it. If this is the case, there is less scope for misunderstanding, and thus less likelihood of plausible allegations that oral statements were relied on. However, the warning needs to be sufficiently highlighted in some way in order to draw it to the tenant's attention. Moreover, the agreement must be drafted in plain intelligible language, or the Tenant will be unable to spot a potential contradiction between what is said and what is printed.' (para 14.1.6)

3. Applicable where the Landlord is a company registered outside of England and Wales or an individual who resides out of England and Wales.

4. Applicable where an agent is appointed to collect the rent and/or manage the Premises on behalf of the Landlord.

5. Applicable where the Premises forms part of a larger building as in the case of a flat.

6. Applicable where the Landlord is a Tenant under a lease. This will, of course, often be the case where the Premises is a flat.

7. The rent payable under an assured shorthold tenancy or an assured tenancy is as agreed between the Landlord and the Tenant, but it should be noted that if the rent exceeds £25,000 a year it takes the tenancy out of the category of assured tenancies, and therefore assured shorthold tenancies and, if the Tenant thinks that the rent is excessive he can refer it to the local rent assessment committee which, if there is a sufficient number of similar lettings and if they are satisfied that the rent charged is significantly higher than the level of rents under such lettings, may determine a rent from such date as it may direct: see the Housing Act 1988, s 22. However, the Tenant may only refer his rent to the committee during the first six months of his period of occupation.

   The periods by reference to which rent is payable are of importance if the Tenant holds over at the end of a fixed term tenancy, whether the periodic tenancy that arises is implied by the common law or by statute. Under the common law, the Tenant under a tenancy agreement for one year at a rent of £x a week who holds over becomes a weekly tenant: *Adler v Blackman* [1953] 1 QB 146, [1952] 2 All ER 945, CA. If the fixed term tenancy is an assured tenancy, at the end of the term the Tenant is entitled to remain in possession under a periodic tenancy the periods of which are the same as those for which the rent was last payable under the fixed term tenancy: see the Housing Act 1988, s 5(2),(3).

8. If the term is longer than three years Form 4 should be used. Care must be taken as to the legal consequences if the date stated for commencement of the term is earlier than the date of the lease. For example, in a lease where provisions were to apply if 50 years of the term had expired, the time was reckoned from the date of the lease and not from an earlier date mentioned from which the term was to run: *Earl of Cadogan v Guinness* [1936] Ch 515, [1936] 2 All ER 29; *Colton v Becollda Property Investments Ltd* [1950] 1 KB 216, CA. The habendum of the lease marks the duration of the tenant's interest so the Landlord has no action for breach of covenant committed before the date of the lease: *Shaw v Kay* (1847) 1 Exch 412.

9. There are a number of circumstances when assured tenancies (and therefore assured shortholds) cannot be created. There include where:

   9A A landlord is a 'resident landlord'.

   9B The rent payable for the exceeds £25,000 per annum.

   9C No rent is payable or the property is in Greater London and the rent payable for the time being under the tenancy is £1,000 or less per year; or outside Greater London and the rent payable for the time being under the tenancy is £250 or less per year.

   9D The parties are entering into a bona fide letting to a company.

10. Careful consideration should be given to rights and reservations. For example, rights relating to access, use of lifts, common areas, communal gardens etc. Reservations may be necessary, for example, to allow a right of way over a garden to access neighbouring land.
11. In the absence of an express provision rent is payable in arrears.
12. Provisions excluding the right of 'set off' are common. The *Guidance on unfair terms in tenancy agreements* (OFT 356, November 2001) says:

> 'Terms which limit or deprive the consumer of access to redress, as well as those which disclaim liability may be considered unfair. One legitimate way for a consumer to obtain compensation from a supplier is to exercise the right to set-off. Where a consumer has an arguable claim under the contract against a supplier, the law generally allows the amount of that claim to be deducted from anything the consumer has to pay. This helps prevent unnecessary legal proceedings.' (para 2.5.1)

> 'If the right of set-off is excluded, tenants may have (or believe they have) no choice but to pay their rent in full, even where they have incurred costs as a result of a breach of an obligation by the landlord. To obtain redress, they then have to go to court. The costs, delays and uncertainties involved may, in practice force them to give up their claim, and deprive them of their rights. The right of set-off should be exercised by tenants only with caution and preferably on legal advice. However, that does not justify terms which stop them from exercising it at all. The OFT does not object to terms that deter tenants from using the right of set-off to withhold excessively large sums.' (paras 2.5.2, 2.5.3)

13. Applicable where the Landlord is a Tenant under a long lease that reserves ground rent, service charge etc.
14. A term that requires the Tenant always to meet charges that could arise through the Landlord's default in carrying out repairing obligations is open to objection see the *Guidance on unfair terms in tenancy agreements* (OFT 356, November 2001) para 2.3.2.
15. Ensure that the repairing obligations of the parties complement each other and suit the type of property and length of term. Where the tenancy is for a short term the Tenant is usually made responsible for the interior, so far a permitted by statue.
16. Regard must be had to the provisions of the Landlord and Tenant Act 1985, ss 11–15.
17. It is usual in a short term tenancy to prohibit alterations or additions to the dwelling and any garden or grounds absolutely.
18. The clause should not be unreasonably restrictive. The *Guidance on unfair terms in tenancy agreements* (OFT 356, November 2001) says:

> 'Terms that ban overnight guests may be seen as producing an unnecessary and unreasonable restriction on normal and harmless use and enjoyment of the property. This term could also cause hardship and suffering, for example, if a tenant's daytime visitor falls ill.' (para 18.8.7, 7th example)

19. It is a term of every assured periodic tenancy that, except with the consent of the landlord, the Tenant must not: (1) assign the tenancy in whole or in part; or (2) sublet or part with possession of the whole or any part of the dwelling house let on the tenancy: see the Housing Act 1988, s 15(1). The Landlord and Tenant Act 1927, s 19 (consent to assign not to be unreasonably withheld etc) is specifically excluded in the case of such implied terms (see the Housing Act 1988, s 15(2)), and the

Landlord may, therefore, refuse consent arbitrarily. It is not, therefore, necessary to include an express prohibition in an agreement for a periodic tenancy that is and always will be an assured tenancy. If an absolute prohibition is required in an assured tenancy this may be included as an express covenant, as permitted by the Housing Act 1988, s 15(3)(a). In the case of a short fixed term an absolute prohibition on dealings is usual.

20. In relation to a total ban on keeping pets, the *Guidance on unfair terms in tenancy agreements* (OFT 356, November 2001) says:

> 'Such a term has been considered unfair under comparable legislation in another EU state because it could prevent a Tenant keeping a goldfish. A term prohibiting the keeping of pets that could harm the property or be a nuisance to other residents would be unlikely to meet the same objection.' (para 18.8.5, 8th example)

21. The agreement should be tailored to ensure that the Landlord has access to fulfil all his obligations as well as to check on the state of the Premises, but rights of entry must not be excessive. The *Guidance on unfair terms in tenancy agreements* (OFT 356, November 2001) says:

> 'A term dealing with rights of entry is unlikely to be challenged if it reflects the ordinary legal position. This recognises that a Landlord who is responsible for carrying out repairs to the property needs reasonable access for two specific purposes: firstly, in order to check whether repairs are necessary, and secondly, to carry them out. Reasonable access means access at reasonable times, and with reasonable notice, except in cases of urgency.' (para 2.7.5)

22. Applicable as with note 6 above. It is advisable given the provisions of the *Guidance of unfair terms in tenancy agreements* (OFT 356, November 2001) that the Tenant is given a copy of any Headlease together with an explanation of the terms if they are at all unclear.

23. Care must be taken to ensure that a Landlord who is a Tenant under a Headlease highlights particular covenants continued in that Lease. This may be the case in the care of Regulations that apply to the Building.

24. The agreement should be tailored to suit the tenant's repairing obligations.

25. For example, consents required under the terms of the Landlord's mortgage or a Landlord's consent required by the terms of the Headlease.

26. The Furniture and Furnishings (Fire) (Safety) Regulations 1988, SI 1988/1324 as amended by SI 1993/207 provide that where furniture or furnishings are supplied 'in the course of business' (but even domestic owners who have never granted a tenancy before are likely to be doing so 'as a business' unless the letting is to a family member) must ensure that such furniture etc complies with the regulations as to fire retardant materials. The covers and the fillings or anything upholstered or which has filling material e g beds, mattresses, headboards, sofas and chairs fitted with loose covers, futons, cushions and pillows, garden furniture and nursery furniture are within the regulations. Items manufactured before 1950, carpets, curtains, duvets and loose covers for mattresses are outside the regulations. Compliance can be proved by manufacturers' labels, receipts for purchase or certificates by interior designers. Failure to comply can result in prosecution by the Trading Standards Office and conviction can result in a fine of up to £5,000 or six months' imprisonment.

27. The Gas Safety (Installation and Use) Regulations 1998, SI 1998/2451 relate to gas

appliances in all let residential properties. All appliances must be tested by a CORGI registered engineer. A Landlord's safety certificate must be provided to the Tenant upon occupation or within 28 days of a certificate or renewal certificate being issued. It is advised that landlords should have additional checks carried out between tenancies. Failure to comply is a criminal offence enforced by Health and Safety Executive and conviction will result in a fine of up to £5,000 or six months' imprisonment.

28. The Electrical Equipment (Safety) Regulations 1994, SI 1994/3260 provides that all electrical appliances and equipment must be tested and a portable appliance test certificate obtained, but there is no provision as to when this has to be done. New electrical appliances usually have a statement as to testing. It is advised that the Landlord should have all appliances tested where it is not evident that this has been done, or re-tested, before the grant of any tenancy agreement. Non-compliance could mean prosecution by the Trading Standards Office and results in a fine of up to £5,000 or six months' imprisonment.

29. The rate of interest should be fair. The *Guidance of unfair terms in tenancy agreements* (OFT 356, November 2001) says:

'A requirement to pay unreasonable interest on arrears of rent, for instance at a rate substantially above the clearing banks' base rates, is likely to be regarded as an unfair penalty. The Tenant would have to pay more than the cost of making up the deficit caused by the tenant's default. A Landlord's personal circumstances may expose him to an interest rate which would normally be considered excessive when passed on to a tenant. In this case, it may not be unfair to require tenants who default on their rent to pay a similar high rate on their arrears provided the reason for this was explained and drawn to their attention at the time of entering into the agreement.' (para 5.2)

30. Notices to quit must then comply with the common law rules and any specific provision in the tenancy agreement. The *Guidance on unfair terms in tenancy agreements* (OFT 356, November 2001) says:

'The law gives residential Tenants considerable protection against arbitrary or immediate termination of their rights of occupation. A court order is required for eviction. The law recognises that Landlords may expressly reserve the right to forfeit in the tenancy agreement. However, terms that appear to reserve a right of forfeiture or re-entry for any breach of covenant (however minor) are apt to mislead the uninformed Tenant. The fact that such terms have long been extensively used does not make them fair. Forfeiture or re-entry clauses need to acknowledge the Tenant's legal rights, at least in general terms, to be more acceptable. They also need to be intelligible to an ordinary person. Terms which do not make it clear that it is unlawful for a Landlord to evict a Tenant and re-enter the property without a court order may be open to objection. Although it may be helpful to advise the Tenant to seek independent legal advice where eviction is threatened, this will not be enough to avoid unfairness if the term does not clearly refer to the need for court proceedings.' (para 18.3.2, 18.3.3)

31. In the absence of these words a formal demand must be served.

32. It may be considerable desirable to extend the events giving rise to a Landlord's right of re-entry. In the case of a company tenant, the events may be extended to the making of an administration order in respect of the company, and any person becoming entitled to exercise the powers conferred on an administrative receiver:

see the Insolvency Act 1986. But if the agreed rent is paid and there is no other material breaches of the lease it is difficult to see why the landlord should be entitled to forfeit the lease on these grounds. The Insolvency Act 1986, s 10(1)(c) provides that after a petition for an administration order has been presented, no proceedings, execution or other legal process may be commenced or continued, and no distress may be levied, against the company or its property except with the leave of the court and subject, where the court gives leave, so such terms as the court may impose. the same applies after an administration order is made (see the Insolvency Act 1986, s 11(3)(d), except that proceedings, execution and process etc may be commenced or continued with the administrator's consent. A landlord wishing to take advantage of the event will have to obtain consent from the administrator or to the court before commencing any proceedings or legal process. It is now clear that such consent is not required as regards a landlord's rights of peaceable re-entry or distraint (see *Re a Debtor (No 13A-IO-1995)* [1996] 1 All ER 691, [1995] 1 WLR 1127) through these will rarely apply to a residential tenancy.

33. The Landlord has the option whether to take advantage of a right of forfeiture or not. If he elects not to do so, the forfeiture is waived. The election may be express or implied, e g if the Landlord does any act by which he recognises that the relationship of Landlord and Tenant is still continuing after the cause of forfeiture has come to his knowledge.

34. The *Guidance on unfair terms in tenancy agreements* (OFT 356, November 2001) says:

'It is central to good faith in any agreement that the parties will keep their word. Good faith demands not only that the parties to a contract are bound by their promises, but also by any other statements they or their representatives make to secure the other person's agreement. If a standard term excludes liability for these unwritten promises and statements, there is considerable scope for prospective tenants to be misled about their rights when the Landlord fails to comply with any obligations or understandings.' (para 14.1.1)

35. Any unfair term does not bind the tenant, but the remainder of the tenancy continues in force if it is capable of continuing in existence without the unfair term: see the Unfair Terms in Consumer Contracts Regulations 1999, SI 1999/2083, reg 8(1),(2).

Form 3
Suggested additional clauses to be included in Form 1 or Form 2; break clauses; option to renew; and simple rent review provisions

[3.1]

3A. Break Clauses

TERMINATION CLAUSE FOR USE IN FORM 1

Landlord's right to terminate

This Assured Shorthold Tenancy may (by virtue of Section 21 of the Housing Act 1988) be brought to an end before the expiry of the Term by notice in writing given by [the Landlord *OR* the Agent] to the Tenant, the length of such notice to be not less than two months provided that such notice does not purport to empower the Landlord to determine this tenancy at any time earlier than [six months from the *insert the date on which the Term commences* or the date of this Agreement, whichever is the later] *OR insert a date later than six months from the later of start date or date of the Agreement*]].[1]

Tenant's right to terminate

This Assured Shorthold Tenancy may be brought to an end before the expiry of the term by notice in writing given by the Tenant to [the Landlord *OR* the Agent] the length of such notice to be not less than [*two months*] provided that such notice does not empower the Tenant to determine this tenancy at any time earlier than [   ] months from the (*insert the date on which the Term commenced*).

TERMINATION FOR USE IN FORM 2

Landlord's right to terminate

This Tenancy may be brought to an end before the expiry of the Term by notice in writing given by [the Landlord *OR* the Agent] the Tenant, the length of such notice to be not less than [*two months*] provided that such notice does not empower the Landlord to determine this tenancy at any time earlier than [   ] months from (*insert the date on which the Term commenced*).

Tenant's right to determine

This Tenancy may be brought to an end before the expiry of the term by notice in writing given by the Tenant to [the Landlord *OR* the Agent], the length of such notice to be not less than [*two months*] provided that such notice does not empower the Tenant to determine this tenancy at any time earlier than [[   ]] months from the (*insert date on which the Term commenced*).

[3.2]

3B.   Option to Renew[2]

Subject to the Tenant having complied with the terms of this Agreement, the tenancy hereby granted may be extended for a further period of [*one year*] commencing on [   ] upon the service by the Tenant of written notice to the Landlord, such notice to be served by the Tenant no later than [   ] whereupon the tenancy created by this Agreement shall be extended for the said period on the same terms and conditions as are contained in this Agreement save:

> that in the definition of 'the Term' in Clause [   ] the words and figures [*delete original Term wording*] shall be substituted for [*insert new Term wording*]
>
> this clause [   ] shall be deleted
>
> [*Break clause may be appropriate*]
>
> [Rent Review may be appropriate: see Form 3C]

[3.3]

3C.   Simple Rent Review Provisions[3]

UPWARDS ONLY REVIEW BY REFERENCE TO THE RETAIL PRICES INDEX

The Rent shall be the rent determined by the provisions of this Clause

In this Clause:

the Initial Rent: means [rent currently stated in the tenancy agreement]

the Review Date: means [date on which parties agree to review the rent]

The Rent shall be determined at the Review Date by multiplying the Initial Rent by the latest [All Items] index value of the Index of Retail Prices published by The Office for National Statistics, or any official publication substituted for it, published before the Review Date and dividing the result by the latest [All Items] index value of the Index published immediately before the date of this Agreement [subject to a minimum increase of [   ]% and a maximum increase of [   ]%]

REVIEW BY REFERENCE TO THE OPEN MARKET VALUE

In this Clause the Rent shall be the rent determined by the provisions of this Clause.

Independent Surveyor: means a surveyor appointed by agreement between the parties or, in the absence of agreement, appointed on the request of either party by the President of the Royal Institution of Chartered Surveyors;

Open Market Rent: means a rent determined in accordance with sub–clause [   ] below;

Prescribed Rate: means [4%] per annum above the Base Rate of [*Bank*] or any other clearing bank the Landlord nominates;

Review Date: means [*date on which parties agree to review rent*].

On each Review Date the Rent shall be reviewed so that on and after the Review Date the Rent shall be the Open Market Rent as at the relevant Review Date (as agreed between the parties or determined by the Independent Surveyor in the absence of agreement as provided below).

The Open Market Rent shall be the best yearly rent at which the Premises might reasonably be expected to be let in the open market.

For the term [   ];

As between a willing Landlord and a willing Tenant, without the Landlord taking a fine or premium;

As a whole with vacant possession;

By an agreement in the same terms in all other respects as this Agreement (save as to the amount of the Rent) but including provisions for rent review on the same terms as those of this Agreement;

It shall be assumed that at the Review Date the obligations on the part of the Landlord and the Tenant have been fully observed and performed;

There shall be disregarded:

> any effect on rent of the fact that the Tenant or any other tenant has been in occupation of the Premises;
>
> any increase in rental value of the Premises due to the existence at the relevant Review Date of any improvement in the Premises carried out otherwise than in pursuance of an obligation to the Landlord or at the request of the Tenant;
>
> in the absence of agreement either party may refer the question of the Open Market Rent to the Independent Surveyor acting as an expert whose decision shall be final and binding on the parties;
>
> if the Rent payable after the Review Date has not been ascertained by the Review Date then:
>
> the Tenant shall continue to pay the Rent at the rate payable immediately before the Review Date such payments being on account of the Rent due after the Review Date;
>
> immediately after the date when the revised Rent is ascertained the Tenant shall pay to the Landlord any shortfall between the revised Rent which would have been payable had it been ascertained by the relevant Review Date ('the shortfall') and the payments made by the Tenant on account together with interest on the shortfall at the [*insert interest rate*] for the period from the date each part of the shortfall arose until the date seven days following the ascertainment of the revised Rent and thereafter at the Prescribed Rate up to the date of payment of the shortfall

Notes to Form 3

1. Although it is no longer the case that an Assured Shorthold Tenancy Agreement need be granted for a term of at least six months, the Landlord cannot however recover possessions under the Housing Act 1988, s 21 during the first six months of the term.

2. Tenancies granted for a short term often contain a right on the part of the Tenant to extend the tenancy for a further period. Care must be taken to ensure that a perpetual right to renew does not exist, hence the need for the words 'the clause [insert number at the clause that gives the Tenant the right to renew] shall be deleted.' An option to renew should not result in the overall term of the tenancy being longer than three years.

3. These rent review clauses are intended to be used for short term residential tenancies (ie less than three years) where provision is to be made for the rent to increase. The most common rent review provision is a review by relevance to the Retail Prices Index but an open market rent review may be preferable where it is important to the Landlord that the rent reflects the rent payable in the open market. These clauses are not suitable for longer tenancies.

Form 4
Lease of house for more than three years but less than seven years – tenant liable for interior repairs, landlord insuring, annual rent review[1]

PARTICULARS
1. DATE OF LEASE [   ]
2. LANDLORD [   ] [company registration No :][of
    [   ] *OR* [whose registered office is
    a[   ]]
3. TENANT [   ] [both] of [   ]
4. DEMISED PREMISES The land, house and premises known as
    [   ] [shown [for the purpose of identification only]
    edged [   ] on the plan annexed to this Lease]
    including all buildings, erections, structures, fixtures, fittings and
    appurtenances on the Demised Premises from time to time; any
    additions, alterations and improvements carried out during the Term;
    and all pipes, sewers, drains, mains, ducts, conduits, gutters, water-
    courses, wires, cables, channels, flues and other connecting media (*or
    as required*) that are in, under or over the Demised Premises and
    further it exclusively, including plant all fixtures and fittings and other
    ancillary apparatus [but excluding the air space above]
5. INITIAL RENT [£   ] a [month (*or as required*)][2]
6. TERM [   ] from and including [   ]

THIS LEASE is made on the date stated in Paragraph 1 of the Particulars

BETWEEN
1. The Landlord specified in Paragraph 2 of the Particulars ('the Land-
    lord'); and
2. The person or persons specified in Paragraph 3 of the Particulars ('the
    Tenant')

[4.1]

1. Definitions and Interpretations
1.1   In this Lease

the Initial Rent: the rent specified in Paragraph 5 of the Particulars

the Demised Premises: the property referred to in Paragraph 4 of the Particulars

the Excepted Rights: the easements rights and privileges specified in Schedule 2 to this Lease[3]

the Included Rights: the easements rights and privileges specified in Schedule 1 to this Lease[3]

the Insurance Rent: the sums payable by the Tenant under the insurance provisions of this Lease

the Landlord: the person mentioned in Paragraph 2 of the Particulars or such other person or persons (if any) entitled from time to time to the reversion immediately expectant upon the determination of the Term

the Rent: the Initial Rent: until the [first] date for review set by Schedule 4 of this Lease and after each review means the sum ascertain in accordance with that Schedule[4]

the Surveyor: the Surveyor for the time being of the Landlord

the Tenant: the person or persons specified in Paragraph 3 of the Particulars which includes the Tenant's personal representatives, administrator or trustee in bankruptcy only[5]

the Term: the term of years specified in Paragraph 6 of the Particulars

1.2   Where any party to this Lease for the time being comprises two or more persons, obligations expressed or implied to be made by or with that party are deemed to be made by or with the persons comprising that party jointly and severally

1.3   Words importing one gender include all genders, words importing the singular include the plural and vice versa, and words importing persons shall be construed as importing a corporate body or a partnership or vice versa

1.4   References to any clause, subclause or schedule without further designation shall be construed as a reference to the clause, subclause or schedule in this Lease so numbered

1.5   The Schedules and the details and descriptions appearing in the Particulars shall be included in and shall form part of this Lease

1.6   The clause, paragraph and schedule headings do not form part of this Lease, and shall not be taken into account in its construction or interpretation

[4.2]

2. Demise and Rent

The Landlord lets[6] to the Tenant [with [full *OR* limited] title guarantee] the Demised Premises TOGETHER WITH the Included Rights but EXCEPT AND RESERVING TO the Landlord the Excepted Rights TO HOLD the Demised Premises to the Tenant for the Term at the Rent and the Insurance Rent

[4.3]

3. Tenant's Covenants

The Tenant covenants with the Landlord as follows:

3.1 To pay rent

3.1.1 To pay the Rent without any deduction or set off[7] by equally [monthly] payments [in advance[8]]

3.1.2 By way of further rent, to pay the Insurance Rent in accordance with Schedule 5

3.1.3 The first payment of the Rent must be made on the date of this Lease and each subsequent payment must be made on [*state days of payment*]

3.1.4 If so required in writing by the Landlord, the Tenant must pay the Rent by banker's order or credit transfer to any bank and account [in the United Kingdom] as the Landlord nominates from time to time

3.1.5 To pay interest at the rate of [   ] on any Rent, Insurance Rent or other sum due under this Lease that is not paid within [   ] of the due date whether formally demanded or not from the date the payment falls due to the date of actual payment whether or not before or after any judgment, the interest is to be recoverable as rent[9]

3.2 To pay outgoings

To pay and discharge all existing and future rates, taxes, duties, charges, assessments, impositions, liabilities and outgoings whatsoever whether parliamentary, parochial, local or of any other description which now or may at any time hereafter be assessed, charged or imposed upon or payable in respect of the Demised Premises or any part or parts thereof or on the owner or occupier in respect thereof respectively

3.3   To pay for services

To pay all charges for gas, water, electricity, telecommunications, fire and security alarms and systems and other services consumed or used at or in relation to the Demised Premises and the meter rents and standing charges for such services

3.4   To pay certain costs

3.4.1   To pay to the Landlord all costs, charges and expenses including solicitors' and counsel's costs and fees and the costs and fees of the Surveyor at any time during the Term incurred by the Landlord in connection with the recovery of arrears of rent or in contemplation of any proceedings in respect of this Lease or under Sections 146 and 147 of the Law of Property Act 1925 or any re-enactment or modification thereof (including all such costs, charges and expenses of and incidental to the preparation and service of a notice under the said sections and of and incidental to any inspection of the Demised Premises and the preparation of any schedule or schedules of dilapidations together with any costs supervising or approving any works of repair), such costs, charges and expenses to be payable notwithstanding that forfeiture is avoided otherwise than by relief granted by the Court and to pay to the Landlord all reasonable costs, charges and expenses of and incidental to any inspection of the Demised Premises and the preparation of any schedule or schedules of dilapidations made at the expiration or sooner determination of the Term together with any costs in supervising or approving any works of repair

3.4.2   To pay all legal costs, expenses and disbursements and the fees of the Surveyor incurred by the Landlord in connection with or resulting from any application by the Tenant for any licence or consent of the Landlord including such costs, expenses, disbursements and fees as shall have accrued when any licence, consent or other matter is refused or any application is withdrawn

3.5   To repair Demised Premises[10]

To keep the interior of the Demised Premises, including door and window frames, glass, locks and fastenings in good condition and repair, except for damage caused by a risk against which the Demised Premises is insured save to the extent that the insurance monies are irrecoverable due to any act or default of the Tenant or anyone under his control. This covenant shall not impose on the Tenant any liability which is imposed on the Landlord notwithstanding any agreement to the contrary by the Landlord & Tenant Act 1985 Sections 11–15 inclusive

3.6   Interior decoration

To redecorate the inside of the Property in the last year of the Term in a good and workmanlike manner, with appropriate materials of good quality to the reasonable satisfaction of the Landlord, any changes in the tints, colours and patterns of the decoration to be approved by the Landlord

3.7   Not to make alterations[11]

3.7.1   Not at any time during the Term to make any external or structural alterations in or additions to the Demised Premises

3.7.2   Not at any time during the Term to make any internal, non-structural alterations in or additions to the Demised Premises [without the Landlord's prior written consent [which consent shall not be unreasonably withheld]]

3.7.3   Not to erect any poles or masts on the Demised Premises or install any cables or wires outside it, whether in connection with telecommunications or otherwise or allow anyone under the Tenant's control to do so

3.7.4   Not, without the consent of the Landlord to affix to or exhibit on the outside of the Demised Premises, or affix or exhibit through any window, or display any where on the Demised Premises, any placard, sign, notice, fascia board or advertisement or allow anyone under the Tenant's control to do so

3.8   Rights of entry for inspection and works[12]

To permit the Landlord and those authorised by the Landlord (and with or without plant, machinery or appliances) at all reasonable times during the Term to enter into and upon the Demised Premises for the purpose of examining the state and condition of the Premises and to ascertain whether the covenants on the part of the Tenant herein contained in this Lease (whether relating to repair or otherwise) are being duly observed and performed and the Tenant will repair and make good all defects of which notice in writing shall be given by the Landlord to the Tenant and for which the Tenant may be liable under this Lease and if the Tenant shall not within one calendar month after the giving of such notice commence and thereafter proceed diligently with the execution of such repairs then it shall be lawful for the Landlord (but without prejudice to the right of re-entry hereinafter contained or to any right or remedy of the Landlord) and those authorised by the Landlord (and with or without appliances, plant or machinery) to enter upon the Demised Premises and execute such repairs and the Tenant shall pay to the Landlord on demand the costs and expenses so incurred by the Landlord (including professional fees)

3.9 Notices

Upon receipt of any notice, order, direction or other thing from any competent authority affecting or likely to affect the Demised Premises or any part thereof forthwith to deliver to the Landlord a true copy of such notice, order, direction or other thing and if so required by the Landlord at the expense of the Landlord to join with the Landlord in making such objection or representation to that or any other appropriate authority or the Court concerning any requirement, proposal or other matter affecting the Demised premises or any part thereof

3.10 Planning requirements

Not at any time to do or permit or suffer to be done any act, matter or thing on or in respect of the Demised Premises which contravenes the provisions of the Town and Country Planning Acts 1990 or any enactment amending or replacing the same and to keep the Landlord indemnified against all claims, demands and liabilities in respect thereof

3.11 To comply with statutes, etc[13]

To comply in all respects at the Tenant's own cost with the provisions of any statute, statutory instrument, rule, order or regulation and of any order, direction or requirement made or given by any authority or the appropriate minister or court so far as the same affect the Demised Premises (whether the same are to be complied with by the Tenant, the owner or the occupier) and forthwith to give notice in writing to the Landlord of the giving of such order, direction or requirement as aforesaid and to keep the Landlord indemnified against all claims, demands and liabilities in respect thereof

3.12 To permit Landlord to affix notice

To permit the Landlord and its agents at any time within three calendar months prior to the expiration or sooner determination of the Term to enter upon the Demised Premises and to affix on any suitable part of the Demised Premises or the exterior of the Building a notice-board for letting or selling the same and not to remove or obscure the said notice-board and to permit all persons by order in writing of the Landlord or its agents to view the Demised Premises without interruption at reasonable hours in the daytime

3.13 Not to give acknowledgements, etc

Not to give to any third party any acknowledgement that the Tenant enjoys any access of light or air to any of the windows or openings in the Demised Premises by the consent of such third party, nor to pay to such third party any sum of money nor to enter into any agreement with such third party for the purpose of inducing or binding such third party to abstain from obstructing the access of light or air to any of the windows or openings in the Demised Premises, and on any of the owners of adjacent land or buildings doing or threatening to do anything which obstructs access of light to any of the windows or openings in the Demised Premises to notify the same forthwith to the Landlord and to permit the Landlord if it so decides to bring all such actions as the Landlord may think fit in the name of the Tenant against any of the owners of the adjacent land in respect of the obstruction of the access of light or air to any of the windows or openings in the Demised Premises, provided always that the Landlord shall indemnify the Tenant against all actions, losses or damage which the Tenant shall suffer by reason of any act or action which the Landlord may do or bring under this Clause 3.15

3.14 User

Not to use or permit the Demised Premises or any part thereof to be used for any trade, business, profession, art or calling or for any illegal or immoral purpose or in any manner which may be or tend to be a source of nuisance, annoyance or damage to the Landlord or their tenants or to the owners or occupiers of any adjacent or neighbouring property nor in any manner save as a private residence in single family occupation only

3.15 To yield up

At the expiration or sooner determination of the Term[14] quietly to yield up unto the Landlord the Demised Premises in such repair and condition as shall in all respects be consistent with full due and timely performance by the Tenant of the covenants on its part contained in this Lease together with all additions and improvements thereof made in the meantime and all fixtures (other than the Tenant's fixtures) in or upon or which during the Term may be placed in or upon the Demised Premises

3.16 To observe regulations

To observe and perform the regulations in Schedule 3 and to ensure that the Tenant's family, visitors, underlessees and licensees also observe and perform such regulations, provided that the Landlord reserve the right to modify or waive such regulations from time to time in its absolute discretion

3.17 To pay Value Added Tax

To pay any Value Added Tax (or tax of a similar nature) properly payable in respect of any rent, costs, fees, charges or expenses payable by the Tenant or which the Tenant is liable to repay to the Landlord or to any other person

3.18 To pay interest[9]

Without prejudice to the rights of the Landlord under any of the covenants or conditions or the proviso for re-entry or otherwise contained in this Lease, to pay to the Landlord interest on any due from the Tenant to the Landlord or to the Surveyor which shall remain unpaid fourteen days after becoming due whether legally demanded or not, such interest to be paid from the date upon which such rent or other sum becomes due for payment to the actual date of payment thereof at the rate of [Four percentage points above the Base Rate of (*Bank*)]

3.19   Insurance

To observe and perform the obligations on the part of the Tenant contained in Schedule 5

3.20   To notify defects

To notify the Landlord upon becoming aware of any defect in the state of the Demised Premises which might (unless remedied) cause personal injury to any person or cause damage to the property of any person, such notification to be given as soon as possible after the existence of any such defect has come to the knowledge of the tenant

3.21   General maintenance

3.21.1   To replace any Landlord's fixtures and fittings in the Demised Premises that are beyond repair at any time during or at the end of the Term

3.21.2   To pay a fair proportion [to be determined in the event of dispute by the Surveyor of the cost of constructing, repairing, rebuilding and cleaning the [party walls, fences, flues, drains, gutters, channels, pipes, wires, entrance ways, roads, pavements (*or as required*)] and other things the use of which is common to the Demised Premises and to any properties. This covenant shall not impose on the Tenant any liability the Landlord and Tenant Act 1985, Sections 11–15 imposes on the Landlord notwithstanding any agreement to the contrary

3.21.3   Not to make any connection with the pipes, sewers or drains in the Demised Premises or extend the wiring except in accordance with plans and specifications approved by the Landlord [whose approval may not be unreasonably withheld] and subject to consent to make the connection or extension having previously been obtained from the competent authority, undertaker or supplier

3.22   Assignment etc[15]

Not to part with possession of the Demised Premises or any part of it; or permit another to occupy it; or hold the Demised Premises on trust for another or assign, sub-let or charge the whole or any part of the Demised Premises

[4.4]

4. Landlord's Covenants

The Landlord covenants with the Tenant as follows:

4.1 Quiet enjoyment[16]

That the Tenant paying the respective rents reserved by this Lease and performing and observing the covenants, conditions and agreements contained in this Lease and on the part of the Tenant to be performed and observed shall peaceably hold and enjoy the Demised Premises (subject to the Excepted Rights) during the Term without any interruption by the Landlord or any person lawfully claiming under or in trust for the Landlord

4.2 Repair

4.2.1   To keep the roof, structure and exterior of the Demised Premises and the [pipes, sewers, drains, mains, ducts, conduits, gutters, wires, cables, channels, flues and other conducting media (*or as required*)] in, on, over, under or serving it, including any ancillary apparatus, in good repair and condition

4.2.2   To keep in repair and proper working order the [central heating and hot water system and other] installations for the supply of water, gas, electricity, for sanitation (including basins, sinks, baths and sanitary conveniences) and for space and water heating.

4.2.3   To comply with the Landlord and Tenant Act 1985, Section 11 as the Landlord's responsibility for repairs in the Demised Premises insofar as the obligations have not been expressly set out in this Clause

4.3 Decoration

To redecorate the outside of the Demised Premises in a good and workmanlike manner and with appropriate materials of good quality as often as is necessary to maintain a [high *OR* good] standard of decorative finish and attractiveness

4.4 Insurance

To observe and perform the obligations on the part of the Landlord contained in Schedule 5 of this Lease

[4.5]

5. Recovery of Possession[17]

5.1   The Landlord's rights under this clause arise if and whenever during this Term:

    5.1.1   the Rent or any part of it or any other sum reserved as rent by this lease lawfully due from the Tenant is unpaid [14 days] after becoming due, whether formally demanded or not[18] or

    5.1.2   the Tenant breaches any covenant, condition or other term of this lease; or

    5.1.3   the Tenant or any person comprised in the Tenant being an individual becomes bankrupt or has an interim receiver appointed in respect of his property; or

    5.1.4   the Tenant being a company enters in to liquidation whether compulsory or voluntary but not if the liquidation is for amalgamation or reconstruction of a solvent company or has a receiver appointed[19]; or

    5.1.5   the Tenant or any person comprised in the Tenant enters into an arrangement for the benefit of his creditors; or

    5.1.6   the Tenant or any person comprised in the Tenant has any distress or execution levied on his goods

even if any previous right of re-entry has been waived[20]

5.2   If and whenever during the Term any of the events in clause 5.1 occurs, the Landlord may bring an action to recover possession from the Tenant and re-enter the Demised Premises, subject:

    5.2.1   in the case of unpaid rent to the Tenant's right to relief on payment of the arrears and costs, and

    5.2.2   in the case of a breach of any obligation other than to pay rent, to his obligations to serve notice on the Tenant specifying the breach complained of, requiring its remedy if it is capable of remedy, and requiring the Tenant to pay compensation in any case, and to allow the Tenant a reasonable time to remedy a breach that is capable of remedy

On the making of a court order for possession this tenancy shall case absolutely but without prejudice to any rights or remedies that may have accrued to the Landlord against the Tenant, or the Tenant against the Landlord in respect of any breach of covenant or other term of this lease including the breach in respect of which the re-entry is made[21]

[4.6]

6. Provisos and Mutual Agreements

6.1 Gas Appliances Safety Regulations[22]

The Landlord has complied with the Gas Safety (Installation and Use) Regulations 1998 and an appropriate gas safety certificate is available at his address for inspection by the Tenant

6.2 Value Added Tax

All sums to be paid by the Tenant under this Lease are expressed exclusive of VAT, and the Tenant must in addition pay the full amount of any VAT or other similar tax on those sums for which the Landlord or other person entitled to the payment of these from time to time are accountable

6.3 Exclusion of Warranties to Use

Nothing in this Lease or any consent granted by the Landlord under this Lease implies or warranties that the Demised Premises may lawfully be used under the Town and Country Planning Act 1990 for a particular use

6.4 Landlord's Details

The Tenant is notified that for the purposes of the Landlord and Tenant Act 1987, Sections 47 and 48 that the name and address of the Landlord is [   ] [that the name and address of the Landlord's in the United Kingdom is [   ]] and that the name and address of the receiver of rent is [   ]

6.5 Rights and easements

By operation of law of the Law of Property Act 1925, Section 62 is excluded from this Lease. The only rights granted to the tenant are those expressly set out in this Lease, and the Tenant is not entitled to any other rights affecting any adjoining property of the Landlord[23]

6.6   Covenants relating to adjoining property

The Tenant is not entitled to the benefit of any covenant, agreement or condition entered into by any tenant of the Landlord in respect of any adjoining property of the Landlord or the right to [enforce] or prevent the release of modification of any such covenant, agreement or condition

6.7   Effective waiver

Each of the Tenant's obligations is to remain in full force both at law and in equity even if the Landlord has waived or released that obligation or waived or released any similar obligation affecting any of his adjoining properties

6.8   Notices

Any notice to be served on the Landlord or the Tenant may be served by registered post, recorded delivery, fax or e-mail. If served on the Landlord, a notice should be served at the address mentioned in clause 6.4 and if served on the Tenant should be served at the Demised Premises or at the address of the Tenant mentioned in the Particulars. Any notice sent by post, in the absence of details of delivery or other recording, shall be deemed to be served on the third working day after posting. Any notice received by fax or by e-mail shall be deemed to be served on the day of transmission if transmitted before 16.30 on a working day, and if transmitted later shall be deemed to have been served on the next following working day ('wording day' in this context means any day from Monday to Friday inclusive other than Christmas Day, Good Friday and any other statutory bank or public holiday)

6.9   Severance clause[24]

If any term of this Lease is, in whole or in part, held to be illegal or unenforceable to any extent under any enactment or rule of law, that term or part shall to that extent be deemed not to form part of this Lease and the enforceability of the remainder of this Lease shall not be affected

6.10   Jurisdiction

The Landlord and the Tenant agree that this Lease shall be exclusively governed by and construed in accordance with the Laws of England and Wales and will submit to the exclusive jurisdiction of the English courts

[4.7]

7. Contracts (Rights of Third Parties) Act 1999

This Lease shall not operate to confer any rights on any third party and no person other than the parties to it may enforce any provision of this Lease by virtue of the Contracts (Rights of Third Parties) Act 1999

[4.8]

8. No Agreement for Lease

It is hereby certified that there is no agreement for lease to which this Lease gives effect

The parties hereto have hereunto set their hands the day and year first before written

[4.9]

SCHEDULE 1

The included rights

1.   If and so long as the Tenant shall punctually make payment of the Rent at the times and in the manner provided in this Lease:

(Insert rights to be granted)

[4.10]

SCHEDULE 2

The excepted rights

(Insert rights to be reserved)

[4.11]

SCHEDULE 3

Regulations

1.   To keep all the windows of the Demised Premises properly cleaned and in particular to clean all the windows at least once in every month

2. To keep the garden that forms part of the Demised Premises (if any) in a neat and tidy condition and not to use the garden or permit the same to be used in a manner which may cause any nuisance or annoyance to the Landlord or their tenants or to the owners or occupiers of any adjoining or neighbouring premises

3. Not to keep or permit to be kept in the Demised Premises any dangerous or offensive goods or materials and not to do or permit to be done anything therein whereby any insurance policy or policies effected on the Demised Premises or on any neighbouring properly may become void or the money payable thereunder reduced or the rate of premium thereon increased and to indemnify and keep the Landlord fully and effectively indemnified against any loss or damage resulting from a breach or non-observance by the Tenant of this regulation

4. Not to keep any animal, reptile or bird in the Demised Premises except with the consent of the Landlord such consent to be revocable in the event of nuisance or annoyance being caused to neighbouring occupiers of if damage is caused to the Demised Premises by the animal bird or reptile[25]

5. Not to place or permit to be placed any burglar alarm, name, advertisement or notice of any description or on the outside of the Demised Premises or in any window thereof nor place nor fix or permit to be placed or fixed any estate agents' board, wireless or television aerial, satellite television dish, wire fitment or any other article on the outside of the Demised Premises, and not to hang or expose any clothes or articles other than curtains inside the Demised Premises so as to be visible from the outside thereof

6. To keep the Property clean and tidy and clear of all rubbish

7. Except for private cars on the drive, not to keep any vehicle, boat, caravan or moveable dwelling on any part of the Demised Premises that is not built on, or store anything on the Demised Premises that is untidy, unclean, unsightly or in any way detrimental to the Demised Premises or the area in which it is located generally

8. Not to change the locks or security codes without the prior written consent of the Landlord. To supply the Landlord with a set of keys or the new code immediately upon replacement. To report immediately to the Landlord if keys or security codes or devices are lost or comprised during the Term and must take immediate steps to provide new keys and/or new security codes or devices supplying the

Landlord with a set of keys or the new code or device immediately upon replacement. To hand-over to the landlord all keys and security devices or codes by 12 noon on the date that the term ends

9. To keep the Demised Premises secure and all fire and security alarms set at all appropriate times

10. To be responsible for any charges levied if the security alarm is set off accidentally by the Tenant or anyone under his control, and all charges for maintenance or repair necessary to resolve the misuse by him or anyone under his control

[4.12]

SCHEDULE 4

Rent review[26]

(Provisions for yearly rent review by reference to the Retail Prices Index)

1. Definitions

In this Schedule

1.1   'the First Review Date' means (*date*), 'the Review Dates means the First Review Date and the date of expiration of each year of the Term, and references to 'a review date' are references to any one of the Review Dates

1.2   'the Initial Rent' means the rent first reserved by this lease; and

1.3   references to 'a review period' are references to a period beginning on any review date and ending on the day before the next review date or the day before the end of the Term as the case may be, and qualified uses of the term are to be construed according

2. Ascertaining the Rent

2.1   The Rent

Until the First Review Date the Rent is to be the Initial Rent and thereafter during each successive review period the Rent is to be a sum equal to [(*where the review is upwards only*) the greater of] the rent payable under this lease immediately before the relevant review date or, if payment of rent has been suspended as provided in this lease, the rent that would have been payable had there been no such suspension or the revised rent that is ascertained in accordance with this schedule

2.2 The Revised Rent

The Rent for any review period is to be determined at the relevant review date by multiplying the Initial Rent by the latest [All Items] index value of the Index of Retail Prices published by the Office for National Statistics or any official publication substituted for it, published before the relevant review date and dividing the result by the latest [All Items] index value of that Index published before the date of this lease

2.3 Changes in the Index

If the reference base used to compile the Index of Retail Prices changes after the date of this lease, the figure taken to be shown in the Index after the change shall be the figure that would have been shown in the Index if the reference base current at the date of this lease had been retained

2.4 Disputes

If it becomes impossible to calculate the Rent for any review period by reference to the Index of Retail prices because of any change in the methods used to compile the Index after the date of this lease or for any other reason whatever, or if any dispute or question whatever arises between the parties as to the amount of the Rent for any review period or the construction or effect of this schedule, the dispute or question is to be determined by a valuer acting as expert who shall have full power to determine on such dates as he deems appropriate what would have been the relevant value had the Index continued on the basis and giving the information assumed to be available for the operation of this schedule

2.5 Calculation of the Rent

2.5.1   The Landlord must obtain copies of the Index of Retail Prices and must supply the Tenant with a copy of the latest publication of the Index before each review date together with calculation of the Rent for the next review period

    2.5.2   Within (*state reasonable period*) of receipt the Tenant must, in writing, acknowledge receipt of the copy and statement and state whether or not he agrees with the calculation

    2.5.3   If the Tenant fails to acknowledge the Landlord's calculation of the Rent with (*state period*) [, or the procedure laid down in this schedule is not complied with,] the Rent for the next review period shall be the amount stated in the Landlord's calculation

    2.5.4   If it is impossible to determine the Rent in accordance with paragraph 2.2, it shall be determined in accordance with paragraph 2.4

3. Payment of the Rent as ascertained

3.1   The Tenant must continue to pay the Initial Rent or the Rent as last reviewed in accordance with the terms of this lease until ascertainment of the revised rent for any review period

3.2   The revised rent for any review period is to be payable from the relevant review date and must be paid until ascertainment of the rent for the next review period or as appropriate for the remainder of the Term

3.3   On ascertainment of the Rent for any review period, the Tenant must forthwith pay to the Landlord the difference between the rent previous payable and the reviewed rent, for the period from the relevant review date to the date of first payment of the revised rent [with interest at the rate of [   ]% above the base lending rate for the time being of (*name of bank*) calculated on a daily basis for that period]

4. Memorandum of new rent

When the Rent for any review period has been ascertained in accordance with this schedule a memorandum of the amount payable, signed by or on behalf of the Landlord and the Tenant, must be annexed to this lease and the counterpart of it. The landlord and the Tenant must bear their own costs in this respect

5. Costs

The Fees and expenses of any valuer appointed to act under this schedule are to be borne equally between the Landlord and the Tenant, unless the valuer considers that either of them has acted unreasonably in which case he may require that party to meet the whole or any part of all fees including the costs of the other party

OR

(Provisions for periodic reviews of rent to the current market value)

1. Definitions

In this schedule

1.1 'the First Review Date' means (*date*), the Review Dates means the First Review Date and the date of expiration of each year of the Term, and references to 'a review date' are references to any one of the Review Dates

1.2 references to 'a review period' are references to a period beginning on any review date and ending on the day before the next review date or the day before the end of the Term as the case may be, and qualified uses of the term are to be construed accordingly

2. Ascertaining the Rent

2.1 The Rent

The rent to be payable after each review date shall be whichever is the higher of the rent payable before the review date and the revised rent ascertained under this schedule

3. The Revised Rent

The revised rent shall be the amount agreed between the Landlord and the Tenant or, if no agreement has been reached [three months] before the relevant review date, an amount to be determined by an independent valuer as provided below

4. Determination by a valuer

4.1 Appointment of the valuer

If the parties fail to agree the revised rent [three months] before the relevant review date, they must refer the matter to an independent chartered surveyor to be nominated by agreement between the Landlord and the Tenant or, in the absence of agreement by or on behalf of the President of the Royal Institution of Chartered Surveyors on the application of the Landlord or the Tenant ('the Valuer')

4.2 Expert

The Valuer shall act as expert and not as arbitrator

4.3 Representations

[Within [one month] of his appointment the Valuer must invite the Landlord and the Tenant to make written representations within [one month] as to the amount of the revised rent and the presumptions set out below supported by comparables and with written evidence of those comparables. [The Valuer must send to each party a copy of the representations and comparables submitted by the other and may invite each party to make further representations within [one month] [*OR*) The parties shall not be entitled to make any submissions except at the Valuer's request]

4.4 Visits

The Valuer may visit the Demised Premises or not at his discretion

4.5 Reasons

The Valuer need not give reasons for his decision unless requested in writing to do so by either party

4.6 Presumptions

The revised rent shall be the open market rent for the Demised Premises for a term of [   ] or the then unexpired residue of the Term whichever is the longer commencing on the relevant review date, on the presumption that as at that date

4.6.1   the Demised Premises is available for letting on the open market without a fine or premium with vacant possession by a willing landlord to a willing

4.6.2   the Demised Premises is to be let as a whole subject to the terms of this Lease other than as to the amount of the rent;

4.6.3   the Demised Premises is fit and available for immediate occupation;

4.6.4   the use of the Demised Premises is residential in accordance with the terms of this Lease; and

4.6.5   the landlord's and tenant's covenants in this Lease have been fully observed and performed

Any effect on the revised rent attributable to the granting of a tenancy to a sitting tenant, any increase in value of the Demised Premises .attributable to an improvement carried out by the Tenant during the Term otherwise than in pursuance of an obligation to the Landlord or in pursuance of an obligation to the Landlord that arose by reference to the consent given for that improvement and any reduction in he value of the Demised Premises attributable to a failure by the Tenant to comply with any terms of this lease, shall be disregarded.

4.7   Time for ascetainment of the revised rent

The Valuer must try to ascertain the amount of the revised rent before the relevant review date and must ascertain it within [one month] after that date

5.   Payment of the new rent

5.1   The Tenant must continue to pay rent at the existing rate in accordance with the terms of this lease until the revised rent is ascertained

5.2   The revised rent for any review period is to be payable from the relevant review date and must be paid until ascertainment of the rent for the next review period or as appropriate for the remainder of the Term

5.3   On ascertainment of the rent for any review period, the Tenant must forthwith pay to the Landlord the difference between the rent previously payable and the revised rent for the period from the relevant review date to the date of first payment of the revised rent [with interest at the rate of [   ]% above the base lending rate for the time being of (*name of bank*) calculated on a daily basis for that period]

6.   Memorandum of the new rent

When the rent for any review period has been ascertained in accordance with this schedule a memorandum of the amount must be endorsed not his lease and the counterpart of it and shall be signed by or on behalf of the Landlord and the Tenant

7. Costs

The fees and expenses of any valuer appointed to act under this schedule shall be borne equally between the Landlord and the Tenant unless the valuer considers that either party has acted unreasonably in which case he may require that party to meet the whole or any part of his fees and the costs of the other party

8. Replacement of the valuer

If the valuer appointed to ascertain the revised rent dies, refused to act or becomes incapable of acting, or if he fails to ascertain the revised rent within (*state period*) of the date on which he accepted the appointment, then if he was appointed by agreement the parties may agree to replace him and appoint a successor. His appointment shall then cease and his successor shall act in accordance with this schedule. If the valuer was appointed by or on behalf of the President of the Royal Institution of Chartered Surveyors either the Landlord or the Tenant may apply to the President to discharge him and appoint another valuer in his place

[4.13]

SCHEDULE 5

Insurance

1.1 Landlord's obligations

1.1.1   The Landlord must keep the Demised Premises insured [in the joint names of the Landlord and the Tenant[27]] unless the insurance is vitiated by any act of the Tenant or anyone under his control. The insurance may be effective in such insurance office or with such underwriters and through such agents as the Landlord from time to time decides

1.1.2   Insurance must be effected for the full cost of rebuilding and reinstating the Demised Premises including VAT, professional fees, shoring-up, debris removal, demolition, site clearance and any works that may be required by statue, and incidental expenses and loss of rent for [three years]

1.1.3   Insurance must be effected against damage or destruction by [fire, storm, tempest, earthquake, lightning, explosion, riot, civil commotion, malicious damage, terrorism, impact by vehicles and by aircraft and articles dropped from aircraft, flood damage and bursting and overflowing of water pipes and tanks (*or as required*)] and by other risks, whether or not of the same nature that the Landlord reasonably decides to insure against from time to time to the extent that such insurance may ordinarily be arranged for properties such as the Demised Premises subject to such excesses, exclusions or limitations as the insurer requires

1.2   Premium

The Insurance Rent shall be the [gross] sums [net of any commission] that the Landlord from time to time pays:

1.2.1   as premium for insuring the Demised Premises , including insuring for loss of rent, as required by this Lease, and

1.2.2   as premium for insuring against liability to third parties arising out of or in connection with any matter relating to the Demised Premises in such amount and on such terms as is reasonable[28]

1.3   Payment

On the date of this lease the Tenant must pay the Insurance Rent for the period beginning on that date and ending on the day before the next policy renewal date. Subsequently the Tenant must pay the Insurance Rent on demand and, if so demanded, in advance of the policy renewal date

1.4   Suspension of the Rent

If and whenever the Demised Premises or any part of it is damaged by any risk against which it is insured so as to be unfit for occupation or use, unless payment of the insurance money is wholly or partly refused because of any act or default of the Tenant or anyone under his control, the Rent, or a fair proportion of it according to the nature and extent of the damage sustained shall be suspended until the Property or the affected part has been rebuilt or reinstated so as to be fit for occupation and use. Any dispute as to the proportion of the Rent suspended or the period of the suspension may be determined in accordance with the Arbitration Act 1996 by an arbitrator to be appointed by agreement between the Landlord and the Tenant or in default by or on behalf of the President for the time being of the Royal Institution of Chartered Surveyors on the application of either the Landlord or the Tenant

1.5   Reinstatement and termination

The Landlord must if practicable reinstate the Demised Premises or any part of it damaged or destroyed by any risk against which it is insured, provided that the damage or destruction was not due to any act or omission of the Tenant or anyone under his control and the insurance policy has not been invalidated by any such act or omission. [If at the end of [six months] from the date of the damage or destruction the property is still not fit for the Tenant's occupation and use either the Landlord or the Tenant may at any time during the following [six months] serve a notice to terminate this lease. On service of such a notice the Term is to cease absolutely but without prejudice to any rights or remedies that may have accrued to either party. [All money received in respect of the insurance effected by the Landlord pursuant to this Lease is to belong to the Landlord absolutely *OR* any money received under the insurance policy effected under this Lease shall be divided between the Landlord and the Tenant in the proportion to the values of their respective interest in the Demised Premises or that part of it at the time of the event giving rise to the payment. In the event of dispute the proportions may be determined under the provisions of the Arbitration Act 1996 as modified or re-enacted from time to time by a single arbitrator to be appointed by agreement between the Landlord and the Tenant or in default of agreement by or on behalf of the President for the time being of the [Royal Institution of Chartered Surveyors] at the request of either party]

1.6   Tenant's further insurance obligations

1.6.1   The Tenant must [permit the Landlord to enter the Demised Premises to carry out any works necessary to]*[29]* comply with all the reasonable requirements and recommendations of the insurers

1.6.2   The Tenant must not do, omit, or allow anything that could cause any insurance policy on or in relation to the Demised Premises to become wholly or partly void or voidable, or do, omit or allow anything by which additional insurance premiums may become payable unless he first notifies the Landlord and agrees to pay the increased premium

1.6.3   If at any time the Demised Premises or any part of it is damaged or destroyed by a risk against which it is insured and the insurance money is wholly or partly irrecoverable because of any act or default of the Tenant or anyone under his control, the Tenant must, at the option of the Landlord either rebuild and reinstate the Demised Premises or the part of it destroyed or damaged or pay the amount or the irrecoverable insurance money to the Landlord on demand

1.7 Landlord's further insurance covenants

1.7.1 The Landlord must produce to the Tenant on demand [a copy of the policy and the last premium renewal receipt (*or as required*) reasonable evidence of the terms of the policy and the fact that the last premium has been paid]

1.7.2 The Landlord must notify the Tenant of any [material]change in the risk covered by the policy from time to time[30]

Notes to Form 4

1. Note that since 28 February 1997 the Housing Act 1988, s 19A as inserted by the Housing Act 1996, s 96(1) provides that all tenancies of residential properties otherwise qualifying, e g for a term of under 21 years at a rent of less than £25,000 a year etc, are considered to be assured shorthold tenancies. Before that date a notice that the tenancy was to be an assured shorthold tenancy had to be served and the tenancy had to be not determinable by the Landlord for at least six months. No prior notice is now required and there is no minimum period requirement. The Landlord cannot, however, recover possession under the Housing Act 1988, s 21 during the first six months of the term.

An assured shorthold tenancy can be created for a fixed term or on a periodic, i e monthly, quarterly etc, basis. The form is for a fixed term.

The *Guidance on unfair terms in tenancy agreements* (OFT 356, November 2001) inter alia says:

'Ordinary words should be used as far as possible, and in their normal sense. However, avoiding the use of technical vocabulary cannot guarantee intelligibility by itself. That also requires clarity in the way terms are organised. Sentences should be short, and the text of the contract should be divided into easily understood sub-headings covering recognisably similar issues. Statutory references, elaborate definitions and extensive cross-referencing between terms should be avoided.' (para 19.7)

'Where a term is ambiguous, a court may be able to find at least one fair meaning in it, and enforce it on that basis, rather than declaring it unfair and void through lack of clarity. However, the Directive makes clear that the 'most favourable interpretation' rule is intended to benefit consumers in private disputes, not to give suppliers a defence against regulatory action (see Regulation 7(2)). If ambiguity in a term could disadvantage tenants it may be challenged as unfair, even if one of its possible meanings is fair.' (para 19.6)

'Fairness is not a matter of rigid prescriptions. The effect of the plain language requirements of the Regulations does not mean that all tenants must understand every word of every contract. Fairness requires that they have a real chance to learn, by the time the contract is binding, about terms that might otherwise disadvantage them. This can be achieved in various ways. Within the contract, significant points can be highlighted and unavoidable technicalities explained. Explanatory material, such as a summary, can also be provided alongside the contract. And information can be conveyed earlier on, in brochures and even advertisements. Preferably, of course, suppliers will use more than one such means.' (para 19.9)

The Tenant would be wise to ascertain whether the Landlord's title is subject to any charges. If it is, the consent of the mortgagees to this agreement should be obtained. Otherwise, the mortgagees are not bound by the agreement and the tenant's possession could be disturbed by the mortgagees seeking possession or exercising their power of sale.

2. The periods by reference to which rent is payable are of importance if the Tenant holds over at the end of a fixed term tenancy, whether the periodic tenancy that arises is implied by the common law or by statute. Under the common law, the Tenant under a tenancy agreement for one year at a rent of £x a week who holds over becomes a weekly tenant: *Adler v Blackman* [1953] 1 QB 146, [1952] 2 All ER 945, CA. If the fixed term tenancy is an assured tenancy, at the end of the term the tenant is entitled to remain in possession under a periodic tenancy the periods of which are the same as those for which rent was last payable under the fixed term tenancy: see the Housing Act 1988, s 5(2),(3).

3. Careful consideration should be given to rights and reservations. For example, rights relating to access, use of lifts, common areas, communal gardens etc. Reservations may be necessary, for example, to allow a right of way over a garden to access neighbouring land.

4. The rent payable under an assured shorthold tenancy or an assured tenancy is as agreed between the Landlord and the Tenant, but it should be noted that if the rent exceeds £25,000 a year it takes the tenancy out of the category of assured tenancies, and therefore assured shorthold tenancies and if the Tenant thinks that the rent is excessive he can refer it to the local rent assessment committee which, if there is a sufficient number of similar lettings and if they are satisfied that the rent charged is significantly higher than the level of rents under such lettings, may determine a rent from such date as it may direct: see the Housing Act 1988, s 22. However, the Tenant may only refer his rent to the committee during the first six months of his period of occupation.

The periods by reference to which rent is payable are of importance if the Tenant holds over at the end of a fixed term tenancy, whether the periodic tenancy that arises is implied by the common law or by statute. Under the common law, the Tenant under a tenancy agreement for one year at a rent of £x a week who holds over becomes a weekly tenant: *Adler v Blackman* [1953] 1 QB 146, [1952] 2 All ER 945, CA. If the fixed term tenancy is an assured tenancy, at the end of the term the Tenant is entitled to remain in possession under a periodic tenancy the periods of which are the same as those for which the rent was last payable under the fixed term tenancy: see the Housing Act 1988, s 5(2),(3).

5. This wording is applicable as the Tenant has no right to assign, sublet or part with possession.

6. The operative word in a lease executed as a deed is traditionally 'demises'. In a lease not executed as a deed 'agrees to let' is commonly used. Any words sufficient to show the parties' intention may be used.

7. Provisions excluding the right of 'set off' are common. The *Guidance on unfair terms in tenancy agreements* (OFT 356, November 2001) says:

> 'Terms which limit or deprive the consumer of access to redress, as well as those which disclaim liability may be considered unfair. One legitimate way for a consumer to obtain compensation from a supplier is to exercise the right to set-off. Where a consumer has an arguable claim under the contract against a supplier, the law generally allows the amount of that claim to be deducted from anything the consumer has to pay. This helps prevent unnecessary legal proceedings.' (para 2.5.1)

> 'If the right of set-off is excluded, tenants may have (or believe they have) no choice but to pay their rent in full, even where they have incurred costs as a result of a breach of an obligation by the landlord. To obtain redress, they then have to go to court. The costs, delays and uncertainties involved may, in practice force them to give up their claim, and deprive them of their rights. The right of set-off should be exercised by tenants only with caution and preferably on legal advice. However, that does not justify terms which stop them from exercising it at all. The OFT does not object to terms that deter tenants from using the right of set-off to withhold excessively large sums.' (paras 2.5.2, 2.5.3)

8. Use the words in square brackets where the rent is to be paid in advance, otherwise rent is taken to be payable in arrears.

9. The rate of interest should be fair. The *Guidance of unfair terms in tenancy agreements* (OFT 356, November 2001) says:

> 'A requirement to pay unreasonable interest on arrears of rent, for instance at a rate substantially above the clearing banks' base rates, is likely to be regarded as an unfair penalty. The Tenant would have to pay more than the cost of making up the deficit caused by the tenant's default. A Landlord's personal circumstances may expose him to an interest rate which would normally be considered excessive when passed on to a tenant. In this case, it may not be unfair to require tenants who default on their rent to pay a similar high rate on their arrears provided the reason for this was explained and drawn to their attention at the time of entering into the agreement.' (para 5.2)

10. Ensure that the repairing obligations of the parties complement each other and suit the type of property and length of term. Where the term is short the Tenant is usually made responsible for the interior, so far as permitted by statute.

11. It is usual in a short term tenancy to prohibit alterations or additions to the dwelling and any garden or grounds absolutely.

12. The agreement should be tailored to ensure that the Landlord has access to fulfil all his obligations as well as to check on the state of the premises, but rights of entry must not be excessive. The *Guidance on unfair terms in tenancy agreements* (OFT 356, November 2001) says:

> 'A term dealing with rights of entry is unlikely to be challenged if it reflects the ordinary legal position. This recognises that a Landlord who is responsible for carrying out repairs to the property needs reasonable access for two specific purposes: firstly, in order to check whether repairs are necessary, and secondly,

to carry them out. Reasonable access means access at reasonable times, and with reasonable notice, except in cases of urgency' (para 2.7.5)

As to serving notice and carrying out works the advantages of this clause for the Landlord must be weighed against the potential liability that it creates under the Defective Premises Act 1972 s4(4) see: *McAuley v Bristol City Council* [1992] QB 134, [1992] 1 All ER 749, CA. It has been held that a claim by the Landlord for recovery of costs under such a clause is a claim for recovery of debt, and can therefore be enforced without requiring leave of the court under the Leasehold Property (Repairs) Act 1938 where it applies: see *Jervis v Harris* [1996] Ch 195, [1996] 1 All ER 303, CA.

13.   The *Guidance on unfair terms in tenancy agreements* (OFT 356, November 2001) says:

> 'A Landlord has a legitimate interest in ensuring that his tenants do not obstruct his compliance with his obligations as a property owner, and may fairly require that they bring to his attention notices that require action on his part. But, this does not justify use of a term, which could force tenants to incur trouble and costs in opposing notices which do not affect their interests, or might even (in the case of notices relating to environmental health) be designed to protect them.' (para 18.8.5, 4th example).

14.   It should be remembered that, if the tenancy is an assured tenancy, when the fixed term expires a statutory periodic tenancy arises which can only be determined by the Landlord on proof of one of the grounds for possession set out in the Housing Act 1988, s 7, Sch 2: see the Housing Act 1988, s 5.

15.   In the case of short terms, an absolute prohibition on dealings is usual. However, the *Guidance on unfair terms in tenancy agreements* (OFT 356, November 2001) says:

> 'Landlords have a legitimate interest in preventing their property from passing into the hands of unsuitable tenants. However, in fixed term tenancies, this does not justify a right to withhold consent to both assignment and subletting arbitrarily. Where tenants are committed to pay rent for a period of months or years, they too have a legitimate interest at stake. If they need to leave, it is not fair of them to be bound to pay rent regardless of the fact that another suitable person is willing and able to do so. For this reason the OFT considers that in fixed term tenancies an absolute ban on both assignment and subletting may be considered unfair. The OFT takes the view that there is unlikely to be an objection to a term which states that the Landlord may prohibit assignment or subletting for a minimum period at the start of the tenancy, for example for the first three months in an agreement of six months or longer.' (para 18.43)

16.   The words 'the Tenant paying the rents reserved by and observing and performing the covenants on his part and the conditions contained in this lease' are frequently included in a covenant for quiet enjoyment, but they have no practical effect and do not make payment of the rent and performance of the covenants into conditions precedent to the operation of the covenant for quiet enjoyment: see *Edge v Boileau* (1885) 52 P&CR 51, CA. The covenant is frequently expressed to apply to 'lawful' interruption by persons 'rightfully' claiming under the Landlord, but it seems that the addition of these words has no practical effect: see *Williams v Gabriel* [1906] 1 KB 155 at 157.

17. This clause is not applicable where the tenancy is or may become an assured shorthold tenancy. It may be used where the tenancy is and will remain outside its statutory protection. The *Guidance on unfair terms in tenancy agreements* (OFT 356, November 2001) says:

> 'The law gives residential tenants considerable protection against arbitrary or immediate termination of their rights of occupation. A court order is required for eviction. The law recognises that landlords may expressly reserve the right to forfeit in the tenancy agreement. However, terms that appear to reserve a right of forfeiture or re-entry for any breach of covenant (however minor) are apt to mislead the uniformed Tenant. The fact that such terms have long been extensively used does not make them fair. Forfeiture or re-entry clauses need to acknowledge the tenant's legal rights, at least in general terms, to be more acceptable. They also need to be intelligible to an ordinary person. Terms which do not make it clear that it is unlawful for a landlord to evict a tenant and re-enter the property without a court order may be open to objection. Although it may be helpful to advise the tenant to seek independent legal advice where eviction is threatened, this will not be enough to avoid unfairness if the term does not clearly refer to the need for court proceedings.' (para 18.3.2, 18.3.3)

18. In the absence of these words a formal demand must be served.

19. It may be considered desirable to extend the events giving rise to a Landlord's right of re-entry. In the case of a company tenant, the events may be extended to the making of an administration order in respect of the company, and any person becoming entitled to exercise the powers conferred on an administrative receiver: see the Insolvency Act 1986. But if the agreed rent is paid and there are no other material breaches of the lease it is difficult to see why the Landlord should be entitled to forfeit the lease on these grounds. The Insolvency Act 1986, s 10(1)(c) provides that after a petition for an administration order has been presented, no proceedings, execution or other legal process may be commenced or continued, and no distress may be levied, against the company or its property except with the leave of the court and subject, where the court give leave, to such terms as the court may impose. The same applies after an administration order is made (see the Insolvency Act 1986, s 11(3)(d)), except that proceedings, execution and process etc may be commenced or continued with the administrator's consent. A Landlord wishing to take advantage of the event will have to obtain consent from the administrator's consent. A Landlord wishing to take advantage of the event will have to obtain consent from the administrator or the court before commencing any proceedings or legal process. It is now clear that such consent is not required as regards a Landlord's right of peaceable re-entry or distraint (see *Re a Debtor (No 13A-IO-1995)* [1996] 1 All ER 691, [1995] 1 WLR 1127) though these will rarely apply to a residential tenancy.

20. The Landlord has the option whether to take advantage of a right of forfeiture or not. If he elects not to do so, the forfeiture is waived. The election may be express or implied, e g if the Landlord does any act by which he recognises that the relationship of Landlord and Tenant is still continuing after the cause of forfeiture has come to his knowledge.

21. The Landlord has a right of actin for existing breaches of covenant event without this express provision : *Hartshorne v Watson* (1838) 4 Bing NC 178; *Blore v Giulini* [1903] 1 KB 356.

22. The Gas Safety (Installation and Use) Regulations 1998, SI 1998/2451 relate to gas

appliances in all let residential properties. All appliances must be tested by a CORGI registered engineer. A Landlord's safety certificate must be provided to the Tenant upon occupation or within 28 days of a certificate or renewal certificate being issued. It is advised that Landlords should have additional checks carried out between tenancies. Failure to comply is a criminal offence enforced by the Health and Safety Executive and conviction will result in a fine of up to £5,000 or six months' imprisonment. Note also that Electrical Equipment (Safety) Regulations 1994, SI 1994/3260 provides that all electrical appliances and equipment must be tested and a portable appliance test certificate obtained, but there is no provision as to when this had be done. New electrical appliances usually have a statement as to testing. It is advised that the Landlord should have all appliances tested where it is not evident that this has been done, or re-tested, before the grant of any tenancy agreement. Non compliance could mean prosecution by the Trading Standards Office and results in a fine of up to £5,000 or six months' imprisonment.

23.   Where the Law of Property Act 1925, s 62 (37 Halsbury's Statutes (4th Edn) Real Property) may operate, it is sensible to define in the lease those rights that are included, and then specifically exclude the operation of that section.

24.   Any term found to be unfair does not bind the Tenant, but the remainder of the tenancy continues in force provided that it is capable of continuing in existence without the unfair term: see the Unfair Terms in Consumer Contracts Regulations 1999, SI 1999/2083 reg 8(1), (2).

25.   In relation to a total ban on keeping pets, the *Guidance of unfair terms in tenancy agreements* (OFT 356), November 2001) says:

> 'Such a term has been considered unfair under comparable legislation in another EU state because it could prevent a tenant keeping a goldfish. A term prohibiting the keeping of pets that could harm the property or be a nuisance to other residents would be unlikely to meet the same objection.' (para 18.8.5, 8th example)

26.   Rent review provisions that determine the increase by reference to objective criteria or as independent valuer are not considered unfair: see the *Guidance on unfair terms in tenancy agreements* (OFT 356, November 2001) (para 12.2).

> 'Terms which permit increases linked to a relevant published price index outside the Landlord's control, such as the RPI, are likely to be acceptable, on paragraph 2(d) of Schedule 2 to the Regulations indicates' (para 12.4)

> 'Also likely to be fair are rent review clauses which allow for an increase in the rent to be determined in the light of objective factors by a person who is independent of the Landlord. A fair alternative, where the parties cannot agree a new rent, is to agree that the matter should be referred to an independent expert' (para 12.4)

27.   In the case of a short term insurance in joint names would be unusual.

28.   This provides should be treated with caution. The *Guidance on unfair terms in tenancy agreements* (OFT 356, November 2001) says:

> 'A contract may be considered unfairly imbalanced if it contains a term making a tenant carry risks that the Landlord is better able to bear. A risk lies more appropriately with the Landlord if it is within his control, or if it is a risk of which the tenant cannot be expected to be aware, or the Landlord can insure against it more cheaply than the Tenant. Terms of particular concern are those

which make the Tenant bear a risk that the Landlord could remove or at least reduce by taking reasonable care in carrying out his obligations, for instance his repairing or fire-safety obligations. Such terms effectively allow the Landlord to be negligent with impunity and are open to objection as exclusion clauses.' (para 18.2.1, 18.2.2)

29. In a lease for between 3 and 7 years a requirement for the tenant himself to comply with requirements that could prove onerous and expensive runs the risk of being found to be unfair on several grounds: see the *Guidance on unfair terms in tenancy agreement* (OFT 356, November 2001) paras 18.1.1, 18.2.1 and 18.8.5.

30. Where insurance in the joint names of the Landlord and the Tenant is not practical, the Tenant should insist that a note of his interest is endorsed on the policy. This protects the Tenant because the insurers should give notice to him of any lapse in the policy and, where it can be shown that the tenant is responsible for the insurance premium under the terms of the lease, it is likely – but not certain – that the insurers would not exercise subrogation rights against the Tenant.

Form 5
Lease of a flat of between 7 and 20 years by reference to a landlord's head lease[1]

PARTICULARS
1. DATE OF SUB-LEASE [   ]
2. LANDLORD [   ] [company Registration No:
    ][of [   ] OR [whose registered
    office is a[   ]]
3. TENANT [   ] [both] of [   ]
4. BUILDING The building known as [   ] of which
    the Property forms part as more particularly described in
    [Clauses [   ]] of the Head Lease
5. DEMISED PREMISES The Flat on the [ ] floor of the Building known
    as [   ] as more particularly described in
    [clauses [   ] of the Head Lease
6. INITIAL RENT [£   ] a [month (or as required)]
7. TERM [   ] from and including
    [   ][2]
8. HEAD LEASE The lease of [   ] dated
    [   ] and made between [parties] for a term of [   ]
    years commencing [   ] [a copy of which is annexed to this
    Sub-lease][3]

THIS SUB-LEASE is made on the date stated in Paragraph 1 of the Particulars

BETWEEN
1. The Landlord specified in Paragraph 2 of the Particulars ('the Landlord'); and
2. The person or persons specified in Paragraph 3 of the Particulars ('the Tenant')

[5.1]

1.   Definitions and Interpretations

1.1   In this Sub-lease

the Initial Rent: the rent specified in Paragraph 6 of the Particulars

the Demised Premises: the property referred to in Paragraph 5 of the Particulars

the Excepted Rights: the easements rights and privileges specified in Schedule 2 to this Sub-lease

the Included Rights: the easements rights and privileges specified in Schedule 1 to this Sub-lease

[**the Insurance Rent**: the sums payable by the Landlord in accordance with his covenant in the Head Lease [*omit if the insurance premium is included in the Head Lease service charge*]

the Landlord: the person mentioned in Paragraph 2 of the Particulars or such other person or persons (if any) entitled from time to time to the reversion immediately expectant upon the determination of the Term

the Rent: the Initial Rent until the [first] date for review set by Schedule 3 of this Lease and after [each] review means the sum ascertain in accordance with that schedule[4]

the Service Charge: the proportion of the service charge under the Head Lease payable by the Landlord in respect of the Demised Premises

the Tenant: the person or persons specified in Paragraph 3 of the Particulars which includes the Tenant's personal representatives, administrator or trustee in bankruptcy only

the Term: the term of years specified in Paragraph 7 of the Particulars

1.2   Where any party to this Lease for the time being comprises two or more persons, obligations expressed or implied to be made by or with that party are deemed to be made by or with the persons comprising that party jointly and severally

1.3   Words importing one gender include all genders, words importing the singular include the plural and vice versa, and words importing persons shall be construed as importing a corporate body or a partnership or vice versa

1.4   References to any clause, sub-clause or schedule without further designation shall be construed as a reference to the clause, subclause or schedule in this Lease so numbered

1.5   The Schedules and the details and descriptions appearing in the Particulars shall be included in and shall form part of this Lease

1.6 References to any right of the Landlord to enter or to have access to the Demised Premises extend to the Head Landlord and anyone the Landlord or Head Landlord authorises, with or without plant or equipment

1.7 Whenever the consent or approval of the Landlord is required, the consent or approval of the Head Landlord acting in its absolute discretion shall also be required and any indemnity or right in favour of the Landlord shall also be in favour of the Head Landlord

1.8 The clause, paragraph and schedule headings do not form part of this Lease, and shall not be taken into account in its construction or interpretation

[5.2]

2. Demise and Rent

The Landlord lets to the Tenant the Demised Premises TOGETHER WITH the Included Rights but EXCEPT AND RESERVING TO the Landlord the Excepted Rights TO HOLD the Demised Premises to the Tenant for the Term at the Rent and [the Insurance Rent] subject to and with the benefit of the matters contained or referred to in the Head Lease

[5.3]

3. Tenant's Covenants

The Tenant covenants with the Landlord as follows:

3.1 To pay rent

3.1.1 To pay the Rent without any deduction or set off[5] by equally [monthly] payments [in advance[6]]

3.1.2 The first payment of the Rent must be made on the date of this Lease and each subsequent payment must be made on [*state days of payment*]

3.1.3 If so required in writing by the Landlord, the Tenant must pay the Rent by banker's order or credit transfer to any bank and account [in the United Kingdom] as the Landlord nominates from time to time

3.1.4 To pay the Service Charge [and Insurance Rent] to the [Head] Landlord on demand [[the Service Charge [and Insurance Rent] demand received from the Head Landlord under the Head Lease having been passed on to the Tenant within [   ] days of receipt of it from the Head Landlord] *OR* [the Tenant having arranged that the Service Charge shall be directly billed to him, the Tenant must make payment at the times and in the manner provided by the Head Lease]]

3.1.5   To pay interest at the rate of [   ] on any Rent, Insurance Rent or other sum due under this Lease that is not paid within [   ] of the due date] whether formally demanded or not from the date the payment falls due to the date of actual payment whether or not before or after any judgment, the interest is to be recoverable as rent[7]

3.2   To pay outgoings

To pay and discharge all existing and future rates, taxes, duties, charges, assessments, impositions, liabilities and outgoings whatsoever whether parliamentary, parochial, local or of any other description which now or may at any time hereafter be assessed, charged or imposed upon or payable in respect of the Demised Premises or any part or parts thereof or on the owner or occupier in respect thereof respectively

3.3   To pay for services

To pay all charges for gas, water, electricity, telecommunications, fire and security alarms and systems and other services consumed or used at or in relation to the Demised Premises and the meter rents and standing charges for such services

3.4   To pay certain costs

3.4.1   To pay to the Landlord all costs, charges and expenses including solicitors' and counsel's costs and fees and the costs and fees of the Surveyor at any time during the Term incurred by the Landlord in connection with the recovery of arrears of rent or in contemplation of any proceedings in respect of this Lease or under Sections 146 and 147 of the Law of Property Act 1925 or any re-enactment or modification thereof (including all such costs, charges and expenses of and incidental to the preparation and service of a notice under the said sections and of and incidental to any inspection of the Demised Premises and the preparation of any schedule or schedules of dilapidations together with any costs supervising or approving any works of repair), such costs, charges and expenses to be payable notwithstanding that forfeiture is avoided otherwise than by relief granted by the Court and to pay to the Landlord all reasonable costs, charges and expenses of and incidental to any inspection of the Demised Premises and the preparation of any schedule or schedules of dilapidations made at the expiration or sooner determination of the Term together with any costs in supervising or approving any works of repair

3.4.2 To pay all legal costs, expenses and disbursements and the fees of the Surveyor incurred by the Landlord in connection with or resulting from any application by the Tenant for any licence or consent of the Landlord including such costs, expenses, disbursements and fees as shall have accrued when any licence, consent or other matter is refused or any application is withdrawn

3.5 Rights of entry for inspection and works

3.5.1 To permit the Landlord to enter the Demised Premises [*provision should reflect the provisions in the Head Lease*] throughout the Term

3.5.2 To permit the Landlord to enter the Demised Premises with any necessary contractors and workmen at all reasonable times upon prior notice and in the event of emergency at any time without notice causing as little inconvenience to the Tenant as reasonably practical and making good any damage caused to the Demised Premises and the Tenant's property to ascertain whether or not the obligations and conditions of this Sub-lease have been observed and performed; to be of the state of repair and condition of the Demised Premises; and following a receipt of a Notice from the Head Landlord, to take any action, including carrying out repairs, decoration and removal of alteration, that is necessary to prevent forfeiture of the Head Lease by the Head Landlord

3.5.3 To permit the Head Landlord to enter the Demised Premises [terms should reflect the Head Lease]

3.5.4   To give notice to the Landlord of any want of repair in the Demised Premises that the Head Landlord is responsible for under the Head Lease in that the landlord's obligations to use his [best/reasonable] endeavours to enforce the provisions of the Head Lease as to the provision of services to the Building and the Demised Premises by the Head Landlord

3.6   Provisions of the Head Lease[8]

3.6.1   To observe and perform the tenant's covenants in the Head Lease [, other than the covenants to pay rents, service charges and other charges reserved by or payable under the Head Lease,] so far as they relate to the Demised Premises, whether or not they are expressly passed on to the Tenant in this Sub-lease and must [indemnify the Landlord against *OR* protect the Landlord from] all damages, claims, costs and expenses arising from breach of those covenants by the Tenant

3.6.2   To pay on demand and on an indemnity basis all costs and expenses the Landlord incurs in enforcing the Head Landlord's covenants in the Head Lease in accordance with Clause [   ] and in obtaining any Head Landlord's consent required under the Head Lease in accordance with Clause [   ] whether or not the application is granted, refused, or granted subject to conditions

3.6.3   To indemnify the Landlord against the consequences of and liability in respect of or arising directly or indirectly out of any breach or non–observance of any of the tenant's covenants contained in the Head Lease

3.7   Notices

Upon receipt of any notice, order, direction or other thing from any competent authority affecting or likely to affect the Demised Premises or any part thereof forthwith to deliver to the Landlord a true copy of such notice, order, direction or other thing and if so required by the Landlord at the expense of the Landlord to join with the Landlord in making such objection or representation to that or any other appropriate authority or the Court concerning any requirement, proposal or other matter affecting the Demised premises or any part thereof

3.8   Planning requirements

Not at any time to do or permit or suffer to be done any act, matter or thing on or in respect of the Demised Premises which contravenes the provisions of the Town and Country Planning Act 1990 or any enactment amending or replacing the same and to keep the Landlord indemnified against all claims, demands and liabilities in respect thereof

3.9   To comply with statutes etc

To comply in all respects at the Tenant's own cost with the provisions of any statute, statutory instrument, rule, order or regulation and of any order, direction or requirement made or given by any authority or the appropriate minister or court so far as the same affect the Demised Premises (whether the same are to be complied with by the Tenant, the owner or the occupier) and forthwith to give notice in writing to the Landlord of the giving of such order, direction or requirement as aforesaid and to keep the Landlord indemnified against all claims, demands and liabilities in respect thereof

3.10   To permit Landlord to affix notice

To permit the Landlord and its agents at any time within three calendar months prior to the expiration or sooner determination of the Term to enter upon the Demised Premises and to affix on any suitable part of the Demised Premises or the exterior of the Building a notice-board for letting or selling the same and not to remove or obscure the said notice-board and to permit all persons by order in writing of the Landlord or its agents to view the Demised Premises without interruption at reasonable hours in the daytime

3.11   To yield up

At the expiration or sooner determination of the Term quietly to yield up unto the Landlord the Demised Premises in such repair and condition as shall in all respects be consistent with full due and timely performance by the Tenant of the covenants on its part contained in this Lease together with all additions and improvements thereof made in the meantime and all fixtures (other than the Tenant's fixtures) in or upon or which during the Term may be placed in or upon the Demised Premises

3.12   To pay Value Added Tax

To pay any Value Added Tax (or tax of a similar nature) properly payable in respect of any rent, costs, fees, charges or expenses payable by the Tenant or which the Tenant is liable to repay to the Landlord or to any other person

3.13   To pay interest

Without prejudice to the rights of the Landlord under any of the covenants or conditions or the proviso for re-entry or otherwise contained in this Lease, to pay to the Landlord interest on any due from the Tenant to the Landlord or to the Surveyor which shall remain unpaid fourteen days after becoming due whether legally demanded or not, such interest to be paid from the date upon which such rent or other sum becomes due for payment to the actual date of payment thereof at the rate of [Four percentage points above the Base Rate of (*Bank*)

3.12   Fixtures and Fittings

To replace any Landlord's fixtures and fittings in the Demised Premises that are beyond repair at any time during or at the end of the Term

[5.4]

4.   Landlord's Covenants

The Landlord covenants with the Tenant as follows:

4.1   Quiet enjoyment

That the Tenant paying the respective rents reserved by this Lease and performing and observing the covenants, conditions and agreements contained in this Lease and on the part of the Tenant to be performed and observed shall peaceably hold and enjoy the Demised Premises (subject to the Excepted Rights) during the Term without any interruption by the Landlord or any person lawfully claiming under or in trust for the Landlord

4.2   Covenants relating to the Head Lease

4.2.1   To pay the rent reserved by the Head Lease at the times and in the manner stated in the Head Lease

4.2.2   To pay the Service Charge at the times and in the manner stated in the Head Lease

4.2.3   To use [best/reasonable endeavours] to ensure that the Head Landlord observes and performs his covenants contained in the Head Lease and must enforce them at the request and cost of the Tenant [subject to the Tenant providing a reasonable sum as security for the Landlord's costs in any legal proceedings undertaken]

4.2.4   To indemnify the Tenant against any breach of the covenants in this Clause 4.2 and against any breach of the covenants of the Head Lease on the tenant's part relating to the Building so far as they do not fall to be performed by the Tenant under this Sub-lease

4.2.5   To use [best/reasonable] endeavours to ensure that the Head Landlord keeps the Building repaired and decorated in accordance with his covenants in the Head Lease

[5.5]

5.   Recovery of Possession

See Clause 5 of Form 4.

[5.6]

6.   Provisos and Mutual Agreements

See Clause 6 of Form 4

[5.7]

7.   Declaration

If the Head Lease is surrendered or merged or otherwise ceases to exist then references to the Head Lease shall have effect as if the Head Lease continued to exist, references to the Head Landlord shall be deemed to refer to the immediate landlord under this Sub-lease and shall be construed as a covenant on the part of the Landlord in terms identical to the covenants on the Head Landlord contained in the Head Lease as if those covenants were expressly set out in this Head Lease in full

[5.8]

8. Contracts (Rights of Third Parties) Act 1999

This Lease shall not operate to confer any rights on any third party and no person other than the parties to it may enforce any provision of this Lease by virtue of the Contracts (Rights of Third Parties) Act 1999

[5.9]

9. No Agreement for Lease

It is hereby certified that there is no agreement for lease to which this Lease gives effect

The parties hereto have hereunto set their hands the day and year first before written

[5.10]

SCHEDULE 1

The included rights

1.   If and so long as the Tenant shall punctually make payment of the Rent at the times and in the manner provided in this Lease:

(Insert rights to be granted – they should reflect the Head Lease)

[5.11]

SCHEDULE 2

The excepted rights

(Insert rights to be reserved – they should reflect the Head Lease)

[5.12]

SCHEDULE 3

Rent review

See the provisions in Schedule 4 of Form 4.

Notes to Form 5

1. Where the term will exceed seven years, it should be noted that, under the Land Registration Act 2002, s 4, a lease granted for such a term will be subject to compulsory registration. The *Guidance on unfair terms in tenancy agreements* (OFT 356, November 2001), *inter alia*, says:

    'Ordinary words should be used as far as possible, and in their normal sense. However, avoiding the use of technical vocabulary cannot guarantee intelligibility by itself. That also requires clarity in the way terms are organised. Sentences should be short, and the text of the contract should be divided into easily understood sub-headings covering recognisably similar issues. Statutory references, elaborate definitions, and extensive cross-referencing between terms should be avoided.' (para 19.7)

    'Where a term is ambiguous, a court may be able to find at least one fair meaning in it, and enforce it on that basis, rather than declaring it unfair and void through lack of clarity. However, the Directive makes clear that the 'most favourable interpretation' rule is intended to benefit consumers in private disputes, not to give suppliers a defence against regulatory action (see Regulation 7(2)). If ambiguity in a term could disadvantage Tenants it may be challenged as unfair, even if one of its possible meanings is fair.' (para 19.6)

    'Fairness is not a matter of rigid prescriptions. The effect of the plain language requirements of the Regulations does not mean that all tenants must understand every word of every contract. Fairness requires that they have a real chance to learn, by the time the contract is binding, about terms that might otherwise disadvantage them. This can be achieved in various ways. Within the contract, significant points can be highlighted, and unavoidable technicalities explained. Explanatory material such as a summary, can be highlighted, and unavoidable technicalities explained. Explanatory material, such as a summary, can also be provided alongside the contract. And information can be conveyed earlier on, in brochures and even advertisements. Preferably, of course, suppliers will use more than one such means.' (para 19.9)

    The Tenant would be wise to ascertain whether the Landlord's title is subject to any charges. If it is, the consent of the mortgagees to this lease should be obtained. Otherwise, the mortgagees are not bound by the agreement and the tenant's possession could be disturbed by the mortgagees seeking possession or exercising their power of sale.

2. The *Guidance on unfair terms in tenancy agreements* (OFT 356, November 2001) says:

    'Terms which bind tenants to unseen obligations are likely to be considered unfair by the OFT. It is a basic requirement of contractual fairness that consumers should always have an opportunity to read and understand terms before becoming bound by them'. (para 9.1)

    One way to demonstrate that a subtenant has had the opportunity to study the head lease terms he must observe is to annex a copy to the sublease.

3. The periods by reference to which rent is payable are of importance if the Tenant holds over at the end of a fixed-term tenancy, whether the periodic tenancy that arises is implied by the common law or by statute. Under the common law, the

Tenant under a tenancy agreement for one year at a rent of £x a week who holds over becomes a weekly tenant: *Adler v Blackman* [1953] 1 QB 146, [1952] 2 All ER 945, CA. If the fixed-term tenancy is an assured tenancy, at the end of the term the Tenant is entitled to remain in possession under a periodic tenancy the periods of which are the same as those for which rent was last payable under the fixed-term tenancy: see the Housing Act 1988, s 5(2), (3).

4.　The rent payable under an assured tenancy is as agreed between the Landlord and the Tenant, but it should be noted that: if the rent exceeds £25,000 a year it takes the tenancy out of the category of assured tenancies and therefore assured shorthold tenancies and if the tenant thinks that the rent is excessive he can refer it to the local rent assessment committee which, if there is a sufficient number of similar lettings and if they are satisfied that the rent charged is significantly higher than the level of rents under such lettings, may determine a rent from such a date as it may direct: see the Housing Act 1988, s 22. However, the Tenant may only refer his rent to the committee during the first six months of his period of occupation.

5.　The *Guidance on unfair terms in tenancy agreements* (OFT 356, November 2001) says:

> 'Terms which limit or deprive the consumer of access to redress, as well as those which disclaim liability may be considered unfair. One legitimate way for a consumer to obtain compensation from a supplier is to exercise the right of set-off. Where a consumer has an arguable claim under the contract against a supplier, the law generally allows the amount of that claim to be deducted from anything the consumer has to pay. This helps prevent unnecessary legal proceedings.' (para 2.5.1)

> 'If the right of set-off is excluded, tenants may have (or believe they have) no choice but to pay their rent in full, even where they have incurred costs as a result of a breach of an obligation by the Landlord. To obtain redress, they then have to go to court. The costs, delays, and uncertainties involved may, in practice, force them to give up their claim, and deprive them of their rights. The right of set-off should be exercised by tenants only with caution and preferably on legal advice. However, that does not justify terms which stop them from exercising it at all. The OFT does not object to terms that deter Tenants from using the right of set-off to withhold excessively large sums.' (paras 2.5.2, 2.5.3)

6.　Use the words in square brackets where the rent is to be paid in advance, otherwise rent is taken to be payable in error.

7.　The rate of interest should be fair. The *Guidance on unfair terms in tenancy agreements* (OFT 356, November 2001) says:

> 'A requirement to pay unreasonable interest on arrears of rent, for instance at a rate substantially above the clearing banks' base rates, is likely to be regarded as an unfair penalty. The Tenant would have to pay more than the cost of making up the deficit caused by the Tenant's default. A Landlord's personal circumstances may expose him to an interest rate which would normally be considered excessive when passed on to a Tenant. In this case, it may not be unfair to require Tenants who default on their rent to pay a similar high rate on their arrears provided the reason for this was explained and drawn to their attention at the time of entering into the agreement.' (para 5.2)

8.　The *Guidance on unfair terms in tenancy agreements* (OFT 356, November 2001) says:

'Tenants may not understand or be aware of the potentially onerous implications of more straightforward technicalities, such as references to 'indemnity' (see para 18.2.6), and the OFT therefore also objects to jargon in all its forms.' (para 19.5)

Form 6
Lease of house for between 7 and 20 years – tenant repairs and insures, rent reviews[1]

PARITICULARS
1. DATE OF LEASE [   ]
2. LANDLORD [   ] [company registration
    No:][of [   ] OR [whose registered
    office is a[   ]]
3. TENANT [   ] [both] of [   ]
4. DEMISED PREMISES The land, house and premises known as
    [   ] [shown [for the purpose of identification only]
    edged [   ] on the plan annexed to this lease]
    including all buildings, erections, structures, fixtures, fittings and
    appurtenances on the Demised Premises from time to time; any
    additions, alterations and improvements carried out during the Term;
    and all pipes, sewers, drains, mains, ducts, conduits, gutters, water-
    courses, wires, cables, channels, flues and other connecting media (or
    as required) that are in, under or over the Demised Premises and
    further it exclusively, including plant all fixtures and fittings and other
    ancillary apparatus [but excluding the air space above]
5. INITIAL RENT [£   ] a [month (or as required)][2]
6. TERM [   ] from and including [   ]

THIS LEASE is made on the date stated in Paragraph 1 of the Particulars
BETWEEN
1. The Landlord specified in Paragraph 2 of the Particulars ('the Land-
    lord'); and
2. The person or persons specified in Paragraph 3 of the Particulars ('the
    Tenant')

[6.1]

1. Definitions and Interpretations

1.1   In this Lease

       the Initial Rent: the rent specified in Paragraph 5 of the Particulars[3]

       the Demised Premises: the property referred to in Paragraph 4 of the
       Particulars[4]

the Excepted Rights: the easements rights and privileges specified in Schedule 2 to this Lease

the Included Rights: the easements rights and privileges specified in Schedule 1 to this Lease

the Landlord: the person mentioned in Paragraph 2 of the Particulars or such other person or persons (if any) entitled from time to time to the reversion immediately expectant upon the determination of the Term

the Rent: the Initial Rent : until the [first] date for review set by Schedule 4 of this Lease and after each review means the sum ascertain in accordance with that Schedule

the Surveyor : the Surveyor for the time being of the Landlord

the Tenant: the person or persons specified in Paragraph 3 of the Particulars which includes [any person or who is for the time being bound by the tenant's obligations in this Lease

the Term : the term of years specified in Paragraph 6 of the Particulars

1.2   Where any party to this Lease for the time being comprises two or more persons, obligations expressed or implied to be made by or with that party are deemed to be made by or with the persons comprising that party jointly and severally

1.3   Words importing one gender include all genders, words importing the singular include the plural and vice versa, and words importing persons shall be construed as importing a corporate body or a partnership or vice versa

1.4   References to any clause, subclause or schedule without further designation shall be construed as a reference to the clause, subclause or schedule in this Lease so numbered

1.5   The Schedules and the details and descriptions appearing in the Particulars shall be included in and shall form part of this Lease

1.6   The clause, paragraph and schedule headings do not form part of this Lease, and shall not be taken into account in its construction or interpretation

[6.2]

2. Demise and Rent

The Landlord lets[5] to the Tenant [with [full *OR* limited] title guarantee] the Demised Premises TOGETHER WITH the Included Rights but EXCEPT

AND RESERVING TO the Landlord the Excepted Rights TO HOLD the Demised Premises to the Tenant for the Term at the Rent

[6.3]

3. Tenant's Covenants

The Tenant covenants with the Landlord as follows:

3.1   To pay rent

3.1.1   To pay the Rent without any deduction or set off[6] by equally [monthly] payments [in advance[7]]

3.1.2   The first payment of the Rent must be made on the date of this Lease and each subsequent payment must be made on [*state days of payment*]

3.1.3   If so required in writing by the Landlord, the Tenant must pay the Rent by banker's order or credit transfer to any bank and account [in the United Kingdom] as the Landlord nominates from time to time

3.1.4   To pay interest at the rate of [   ] on any Rent or other sum due under this Lease that is not paid within [   ] of the due date whether formally demanded or not from the date the payment falls due to the date of actual payment whether or not before or after any judgment, the interest is to be recoverable as rent[8]

3.2   To pay outgoings

To pay and discharge all existing and future rates, taxes, duties, charges, assessments, impositions, liabilities and outgoings whatsoever whether parliamentary, parochial, local or of any other description which now or may at any time hereafter be assessed, charged or imposed upon or payable in respect of the Demised Premises or any part or parts thereof or on the owner or occupier in respect thereof respectively

3.3   To pay for services

To pay all charges for gas, water, electricity, telecommunications, fire and security alarms and systems and other services consumed or used at or in relation to the Demised Premises and the meter rents and standing charges for such services

3.4   To pay certain costs

3.4.1   To pay to the Landlord all costs, charges and expenses including solicitors' and counsel's costs and fees and the costs and fees of the Surveyor at any time during the Term incurred by the Landlord in connection with the recovery of arrears of rent or in contemplation of any proceedings in respect of this Lease or under Sections 146 and 147 of the Law of Property Act 1925 or any re-enactment or modification thereof (including all such costs, charges and expenses of and incidental to the preparation and service of a notice under the said sections and of and incidental to any inspection of the Demised Premises and the preparation of any schedule or schedules of dilapidations together with any costs supervising or approving any works of repair), such costs, charges and expenses to be payable notwithstanding that forfeiture is avoided otherwise than by relief granted by the Court and to pay to the Landlord all reasonable costs, charges and expenses of and incidental to any inspection of the Demised Premises and the preparation of any schedule or schedules of dilapidations made at the expiration or sooner determination of the Term together with any costs in supervising or approving any works of repair

3.4.2   To pay all legal costs, expenses and disbursements and the fees of the Surveyor incurred by the Landlord in connection with or resulting from any application by the Tenant for any licence or consent of the Landlord including such costs, expenses, disbursements and fees as shall have accrued when any licence, consent or other matter is refused or any application is withdrawn

3.5   To repair Demised Premises

To keep the Demised Premises in good and tenantable repair and condition[9]

3.6   Decoration

3.6.1   In every [fifth] year of the Term and in the last year of the Term (howsoever determined) to paint with two coats of paint and to paper, varnish, colour, grain and whitewash all the inside parts of the Demised Premises and also the internal surfaces of the doors, door frames and window frames fitted in the walls bounding the Demised Premises as have been or ought properly to be so painted, papered, varnished, coloured, grained and whitewashed in a good and workmanlike manner with materials of good quality [to the reasonable satisfaction of the Landlord]. [The colours, patterns and materials used in the last year of the Term to be approved by the Landlord] [whose approval may not be unreasonably withheld].]

3.6.2   In every [third] year of the Term and in the last year of the Term to redecorate the exterior of the Demised Premises including the external surfaces of the doors, door frames and window frames in a good and workmanlike manner with appropriate materials of good quality in colours and types as the Landlord [reasonably] requires.

3.7   Not to make alterations

3.7.1   Not at any time during the Term to make any external or structural alterations in or additions to the Demised Premises

3.7.2   Not at any time during the Term to make any internal, non-structural alterations in or additions to the Demised Premises [without the Landlord's prior written consent [which consent shall not be unreasonably withheld]]

3.7.3   Not to erect any poles or masts on the Demised Premises or install any cables or wires outside it, whether in connection with telecommunications or otherwise or allow anyone under the Tenant's control to do so

3.7.4   Not, without the consent of the Landlord to affix to or exhibit on the outside of the Demised Premises, or affix or exhibit through any window, or display any where on the Demised Premises, any placard, sign, notice, fascia board or advertisement or allow anyone under the Tenant's control to do so

3.8   Rights of entry for inspection and works[10]

To permit the Landlord and those authorised by the Landlord (and with or without plant, machinery or appliances) at all reasonable times during the Term to enter into and upon the Demised Premises for the purpose of examining the state and condition of the Premises and to ascertain whether the covenants on the part of the Tenant herein contained in this Lease (whether relating to repair or otherwise) are being duly observed and performed and the Tenant will repair and make good all defects of which notice in writing shall be given by the Landlord to the Tenant and for which the Tenant may be liable under this Lease and if the Tenant shall not within one calendar month after the giving of such notice commence and thereafter proceed diligently with the execution of such repairs then it shall be lawful for the Landlord (but without prejudice to the right of re-entry hereinafter contained or to any right or remedy of the Landlord) and those authorised by the Landlord (and with or without appliances, plant or machinery) to enter upon the Demised Premises and execute such repairs and the Tenant shall pay to the Landlord on demand the costs and expenses so incurred by the Landlord (including professional fees)

3.9   Notices[11]

Upon receipt of any notice, order, direction or other thing from any competent authority affecting or likely to affect the Demised Premises or any part thereof forthwith to deliver to the Landlord a true copy of such notice, order, direction or other thing and if so required by the Landlord at the expense of the Landlord to join with the Landlord in making such objection or representation to that or any other appropriate authority or the Court concerning any requirement, proposal or other matter affecting the Demised premises or any part thereof

3.10   Planning requirements

Not at any time to do or permit or suffer to be done any act, matter or thing on or in respect of the Demised Premises which contravenes the provisions of the Town and Country Planning Acts 1990 or any enactment amending or replacing the same and to keep the Landlord indemnified against all claims, demands and liabilities in respect thereof

3.11   To comply with statutes, etc

To comply in all respects at the Tenant's own cost with the provisions of any statute, statutory instrument, rule, order or regulation and of any order, direction or requirement made or given by any authority or the appropriate minister or court so far as the same affect the Demised Premises (whether the same are to be complied with by the Tenant, the owner or the occupier) and forthwith to give notice in writing to the Landlord of the giving of such order, direction or requirement as aforesaid and to keep the Landlord indemnified against all claims, demands and liabilities in respect thereof

3.12   To permit Landlord to affix notice

To permit the Landlord and its agents at any time within three calendar months prior to the expiration or sooner determination of the Term to enter upon the Demised Premises and to affix on any suitable part of the Demised Premises or the exterior of the Building a notice-board for letting or selling the same and not to remove or obscure the said notice-board and to permit all persons by order in writing of the Landlord or its agents to view the Demised Premises without interruption at reasonable hours in the daytime

3.13   Not to give acknowledgements, etc

Not to give to any third party any acknowledgement that the Tenant enjoys any access of light or air to any of the windows or openings in the Demised Premises by the consent of such third party, nor to pay to such third party any sum of money nor to enter into any agreement with such third party for the purpose of inducing or binding such third party to abstain from obstructing the access of light or air to any of the windows or openings in the Demised Premises, and on any of the owners of adjacent land or buildings doing or threatening to do anything which obstructs access of light to any of the windows or openings in the Demised Premises to notify the same forthwith to the Landlord and to permit the Landlord if it so decides to bring all such actions as the Landlord may think fit in the name of the Tenant against any of the owners of the adjacent land in respect of the obstruction of the access of light or air to any of the windows or openings in the Demised Premises, provided always that the Landlord shall indemnify the Tenant against all actions, losses or damage which the Tenant shall suffer by reason of any act or action which the Landlord may do or bring under this Clause 3.15

3.14   User

Not to use or permit the Demised Premises or any part thereof to be used for any trade, business, profession, art or calling or for any illegal or immoral purpose or in any manner which may be or tend to be a source of nuisance, annoyance or damage to the Landlord or their tenants or to the owners or occupiers of any adjacent or neighbouring property nor in any manner save as a private residence in single family occupation only

3.15 To yield up[12]

At the expiration or sooner determination of the Term quietly to yield up unto the Landlord the Demised Premises in such repair and condition as shall in all respects be consistent with full due and timely performance by the Tenant of the covenants on its part contained in this Lease together with all additions and improvements thereof made in the meantime and all fixtures (other than the Tenant's fixtures) in or upon or which during the Term may be placed in or upon the Demised Premises

3.16 To observe regulations

To observe and perform the regulations in Schedule 3 and to ensure that the Tenant's family, visitors, underleasees and licensees also observe and perform such regulations, provided that the Landlord reserve the right to modify or waive such regulations from time to time in its absolute discretion

3.17 To pay Value Added Tax

To pay any Value Added Tax (or tax of a similar nature) properly payable in respect of any rent, costs, fees, charges or expenses payable by the Tenant or which the Tenant is liable to repay to the Landlord or to any other person

3.18 To pay interest

Without prejudice to the rights of the Landlord under any of the covenants or conditions or the proviso for re-entry or otherwise contained in this Lease, to pay to the Landlord interest on any due from the Tenant to the Landlord or to the Surveyor which shall remain unpaid fourteen days after becoming due whether legally demanded or not, such interest to be paid from the date upon which such rent or other sum becomes due for payment to the actual date of payment thereof at the rate of [Four percentage points above the Base Rate of *(Bank)*][8]

3.19   Insurance

To observe and perform the obligations on the part of the Tenant contained in Schedule 5

3.20   To notify defects

To notify the Landlord upon becoming aware of any defect in the state of the Demised Premises which might (unless remedied) cause personal injury to any person or cause damage to the property of any person, such notification to be given as soon as possible after the existence of any such defect has come to the knowledge of the tenant

3.21   General maintenance

3.21.1   To pay a fair proportion [to be determined in the event of dispute by the Surveyor of the cost of constructing, repairing, rebuilding and cleaning the [party walls, fences, flues, drains, gutters, channels, pipes, wires, entrance ways, roads, pavements (*or as required*)] and other things the use of which is common to the Demised Premises and to any properties

3.21.2   Not to make any connection with the pipes, sewers or drains in the Demised Premises or extend the wiring except in accordance with plans and specifications approved by the Landlord [whose approval may not be unreasonably withheld] and subject to consent to make the connection or extension having previously been obtained from the competent authority, undertaker or supplier

3.22   Assignment, etc

3.22.1   Not to assign, sub-let or part with possession of part only of the Demised Premises

3.22.2   Not to part with possession of the Demised Premises or any part of it or permit another person to occupy it or any part of it otherwise than as a visitor, except pursuant to a transaction permitted by and effected in accordance with the provisions of this Lease; or hold the Demised Premises on trust for another

3.22.3   The Tenant may assign [sub-let[13]] or charge the whole of the Demised Premises [provided that the Tenant and the proposed assignee have entered into a licence to assign containing an authorised guarantee agreement the rent or other sums due under this Lease have been paid up to the date of the assignment in the reasonable opinion of the Landlord the proposed assignee is of sufficient financial standing to pay the rent and to meet the liabilities of the tenant under this Lease; and any sub-lease complies with the provisions of Clause 3.24.4 and subject to obtaining the Landlord's previous written consent, which may not be unreasonably withheld [or delayed][14]

3.22.4   Every permitted sub-lease must be granted, without a fine or premium. The rent must not be less than the greater of the then open market rent for the Demised Premises and the Rent under this Lease, and must be payable in advance on the days on which the Rent is payable under this Lease. Every sub-lease must contain provisions for the upwards only review of the rent reserved by it, on the basis and on the review dates set out in this Lease prohibiting the sub-tenant from doing or allowing anything in relation to the Demised Premises inconsistent with or in breach of the provisions of this Lease for re-entry by the sub-landlord on breach of any covenant by the sub-tenant imposing an absolute prohibition against all dealings with the Demised Premises other than assignment [or charging] of the whole; prohibiting assignment [or charging] of the whole of the Demised Premises without the consent of the Landlord under this Lease requiring the assignee on any assignment of the sub-lease to enter into direct covenants with the Landlord to the same effect as those contained in this Lease requiring on each assignment of the sub-lease that the assignor enters into an authorised guarantee agreement in favour of the Landlord prohibiting the sub-tenant from holding on trust for another or permitting another to share or occupy the whole or any part of the Demised Premises; and imposing in relation to any permitted assignment, [or charge] the same obligations for registration with the Landlord as are contained in this Lease in relation to dispositions by the Tenant

3.22.5   Before any permitted sub-letting, the Tenant must ensure that the sub-tenant enters into a direct covenant with the Landlord that, while the sub-tenant is bound by the tenant covenants of the sub-lease and while he is bound by an authorised guarantee agreement, the sub-tenant will observe and perform the tenant covenants contained in this Lease except the covenant to pay the rent reserved by this Lease and in that sub-lease

3.22.6   The Tenant must enforce the performance and observance of the provisions of any permitted sub-lease by every sub-tenant, and must not either expressly or by implication waive any breach of the covenants or conditions on the part of any sub-tenant or assignee of a sub-lease. The Tenant must not vary the terms or accept a surrender of any permitted sub-lease without the consent of the Landlord, whose consent may not be unreasonably withheld or delayed

3.22.7.1 The Tenant must ensure that the rent of any permitted sub-lease is reviewed in accordance with the terms of the sub-lease

3.22.7.2 The Tenant must not agree the reviewed rent with the sub-tenant without the approval of the Landlord

3.22.7.3 Where the sub-lease provides such an option, the Tenant must not, without the approval of the Landlord, agree whether the third party determining the revised rent in default of agreement should act as an arbitrator or as an expert

3.22.7.4 The Tenant must not, without the approval of the Landlord, agree the appointment of a person to act as the third party determining the revised rent

3.22.7.5 The Tenant must give written notice of any assignment [, sub-letting] or charge of the Demised Premises to the Landlord within [1 month] of its date, and forward a certified copy of the instrument to the Landlord's solicitors together with [the registration fee of £[   ] *or*) their reasonable registration fee], plus VAT if not recoverable by the Landlord, in respect of each such document. At all times during the Term the Tenant must give the Landlord or his solicitors in writing on written request the name, address and other reasonably required details of any person to whom a derivative interest in the Demised Premises has been granted

3.23 To permit [on reasonable notice] at any time during the Term, prospective purchasers of the Landlord's reversion or any other interest superior to the Term, or agents instructed in connection with the sale of the reversion or such an interest, to view the Demised Premises by appointment

[6.4]

4. Landlord's Covenants

The Landlord covenants with the Tenant as follows:

Quiet Enjoyment[16]

That the Tenant paying the respective rents reserved by this Lease and performing and observing the covenants, conditions and agreements contained in this Lease and on the part of the Tenant to be performed and observed shall peaceably hold and enjoy the Demised Premises (subject to the Excepted Rights) during the Term without any interruption by the Landlord or any person lawfully claiming under or in trust for the Landlord

[6.5]

5. Recovery of Possession[17]

5.1 The Landlord's rights under this clause arise if and whenever during the Term:

    5.1.1 the Rent or any part of it or any other sum reserved as rent by this Lease lawfully due from the Tenant is unpaid [14 days] after becoming due, whether formally demanded or not or[18]

    5.1.2 the Tenant breaches any covenant, condition or other term of this Lease; or

    5.1.3 the Tenant or any person comprised in the Tenant being an individual becomes bankrupt or has an interim receiver appointed in respect of his property; or

    5.1.4 the Tenant being a company enters into liquidation whether compulsory or voluntary but not if the liquidation is for amalgamation or reconstruction of a solvent company or has a receiver appointed[19]; or

5.1.5   the Tenant or any person comprised in the Tenant enters into an arrangement for the benefit of his creditors; or

5.1.6   the Tenant or any person comprised in the Tenant has any distress or execution levied on his goods[20]

even if any previous right of re-entry has been waived[21]

5.2   If and whenever during the Term any of the events in clause 5.1 occurs, the Landlord may bring an action to recover possession from the Tenant and re-enter the Demised Premises, subject:

5.2.1   in the case of unpaid rent to the Tenant's right to relief on payment of the arrears and costs, and

5.2.2   in the case of a breach of any obligation other than to pay rent, to his obligations to serve notice on the Tenant specifying the breach complained of, requiring its remedy if it is capable of remedy, and requiring the Tenant to pay compensation in any case, and to allow the Tenant a reasonable time to remedy a breach that is capable of remedy

On the making of a court order for possession this tenancy shall cease absolutely but without prejudice to any rights or remedies that may have accrued to the Landlord against the Tenant, or the Tenant against the Landlord in respect of any breach of covenant or other term of this Lease including the breach in respect of which the re-entry is made

[6.6]

6.   Provisos and Mutual Agreements

6.1   Gas Appliances Safety Regulations

The Landlord has complied with the Gas Safety (Installation and Use) Regulations 1998 and an appropriate gas safety certificate is available at his address for inspection by the Tenant

6.2   Value Added Tax

All sums to be paid by the Tenant under this Lease are expressed exclusive of VAT, and the Tenant must in addition pay the full amount of any VAT or other similar tax on those sums for which the Landlord or other person entitled to the payment of these from time to time are accountable

6.3   **Exclusion of warranties to use**

Nothing in this Lease or any consent granted by the Landlord under this Lease implies or warrants that the Demised Premises may lawfully be used under the Town and Country Planning Act 1990 for a particular use

6.4   **Landlord's details**

The Tenant is notified that for the purposes of the Landlord and Tenant Act 1987, Sections 47 and 48 the name and address of the Landlord is [   ] [the name and address of the Landlord in the United Kingdom is [   ]] and the name and address of the receiver of rent is [   ]

6.5   **Rights and Easements**[22]

By operation of law of the Law of Property Act 1925, Section 62 is excluded from this Lease. The only rights granted to the Tenant are those expressly set out in this Lease, and the Tenant is not entitled to any other rights affecting any adjoining property of the Landlord

6.6   **Covenants relating to adjoining property**

The Tenant is not entitled to the benefit of any covenant, agreement or condition entered into by any tenant of the Landlord in respect of any adjoining property of the Landlord or the right to [enforce or] prevent the release or modification of any such covenant, agreement or condition

6.7   **Effective waiver**

Each of the Tenant's obligations is to remain in full force both at law and in equity even if the Landlord has waived or released that obligation or waived or released any similar obligation affecting any of his adjoining properties

6.8   **Notices**

Any notice to be served on the Landlord or the Tenant may be served by registered post, recorded delivery, fax or e-mail. If served on the Landlord, a notice should be served at the address mentioned in clause 6.4 and if served on the Tenant should be served at the Demised Premises or at the address of the Tenant mentioned in the Particulars. Any notice sent by post, in the absence of details of delivery or other recording, shall be deemed to be served on the third working day after posting. Any notice received by fax or by e-mail shall be deemed to be served on the day of transmission if transmitted before 16.30 on a working day, and if transmitted later shall be deemed to have been served on the next following working day ('working day' in this context means any day from Monday to Friday inclusive other than Christmas Day, Good Friday and any other statutory bank or public holiday)

6.9   Severance clause[23]

If any term of this Lease is, in whole or in part, held to be illegal or unenforceable to any extent under any enactment or rule of law, that term or part shall to that extent be deemed not to form part of this Lease and the enforceability of the remainder of this Lease shall not be affected

6.10   Jurisdiction

The Landlord and the Tenant agree that this Lease shall be exclusively governed by and construed in accordance with the Laws of England and Wales and will submit to the exclusive jurisdiction of the English courts

[6.7]

7.   Contracts (Rights of Third Parties) Act 1999

This Lease shall not operate to confer any rights on any third party and no person other than the parties to it may enforce any provision of this Lease by virtue of the Contracts (Rights of Third Parties) Act 1999

[6.8]

8.   No Agreement for Lease

It is hereby certified that there is no agreement for lease to which this Lease gives effect

The parties hereto have hereunto set their hands the day and year first before written

[6.9]

SCHEDULE 1

The included rights

1.   If and so long as the Tenant shall punctually make payment of the Rent at the times and in the manner provided in this Lease:

(Insert rights to be granted)

[6.10]

SCHEDULE 2

The excepted rights

(Insert rights to be reserved)

[6.11]

SCHEDULE 3

Regulations

1.   To keep all the windows of the Demised Premises properly cleaned and in particular to clean all the windows at least once in every month

2.   To keep the garden that forms part of the Demised Premises (if any) in a neat and tidy condition and not to use the garden or permit the same to be used in a manner which may cause any nuisance or annoyance to the Landlord or their tenants or to the owners or occupiers of any adjoining or neighbouring premises

3.   Not to keep or permit to be kept in the Demised Premises any dangerous or offensive goods or materials and not to do or permit to be done anything therein whereby any insurance policy or policies effected on the Demised Premises or on any neighbouring property may become void or the money payable thereunder reduced or the rate of premium thereon increased and to indemnify and keep the Landlord fully and effectively indemnified against any loss or damage resulting from a breach or non-observance by the Tenant of this regulation

4. Not to keep any animal, reptile or bird in the Demised Premises except with the consent of the Landlord such consent to be revocable in the event of nuisance or annoyance being caused to neighbouring occupiers of if damage is caused to the Demised Premises by the animal bird or reptile[24]

5. Not to place or permit to be placed any burglar alarm, name, advertisement or notice of any description on the outside of the Demised Premises or in any window thereof nor place nor fix or permit to be placed or fixed any estate agents' board, wireless or television aerial, satellite television dish, wire fitment or any other article on the outside of the Demised Premises and not to hang or expose any clothes or articles other than curtains inside the Demised Premises so as to be visible from the outside thereof

6. To keep the Demised Premises clean and tidy and clear of all rubbish

7. Except for private cars on the drive, not to keep any vehicle, boat, caravan or movable dwelling on any part of the Demised Premises that is not built on, or store anything on the Demised Premises that is untidy, unclean, unsightly or in any way detrimental to the Demised Premises or the area in which it is located generally

8. Not to change the locks or security codes without the prior written consent of the Landlord. To supply the Landlord with a set of keys or the new code immediately upon replacement. To report immediately to the Landlord if keys or security codes or devices are lost or comprised during the Term and must take immediate steps to provide new keys and/or new security codes or devices supplying the Landlord with a set of keys or the new code or device immediately upon replacement. To handover to the landlord all keys and security devices or codes by 12 noon on the date that the Term ends

9. To keep the Demised Premises secure and all fire and security alarms set at all appropriate times

10. To be responsible for any charges levied if the security alarm is set off accidentally by the Tenant or anyone under his control, and all charges for maintenance or repair necessary to resolve the misuse by him or anyone under his control

[6.12]

SCHEDULE 4

Rent review[25]

1. Definitions

In this schedule

    1.1   'the First Review Date' means (*date*), 'the Review Dates' means the First Review Date and [*dates*], and references to 'a review date' are references to any one of the Review Dates

    1.2   references to 'a review period' are references to a period beginning on any review date and ending on the day before the next review date or the day before the end of the Term as the case may be, and qualified uses of the term are to be construed accordingly

2. Ascertaining the Rent

2.1 The Rent

The rent to be payable after each review date shall be whichever is the higher of the rent payable before the review date and the revised rent ascertained under this schedule

2.2 The Revised Rent

The revised rent shall be the amount agreed between the Landlord and the Tenant or, if no agreement has been reached [three months] before the relevant review date, an amount to be determined by an independent valuer as provided below

3. Determination by a valuer

3.1 Appointment of the valuer

If the parties fail to agree the revised rent [three months] before the relevant review date, they must refer the matter to an independent chartered surveyor to be nominated by agreement between the Landlord and the Tenant or, in the absence of agreement, by or on behalf of the President of the Royal Institution of Chartered Surveyors on the application of the Landlord or the Tenant ('the Valuer')

3.2 Expert

The Valuer shall act as expert and not as arbitrator

3.3 Representations

[Within [1 month] of his appointment the Valuer must invite the Landlord and the Tenant to make written representations within [one month] as to the amount of the revised rent and the presumptions set out below supported by comparables and with written evidence of those comparables. [The Valuer must send to each party a copy of the representations and comparables submitted by the other and may invite each party to make further representations within [one month] [*OR*) The parties shall not be entitled to make any submissions except at the Valuer's request]

3.4 Visits

The Valuer may visit the Demised Premises or not at his discretion

3.5 Reasons

The Valuer need not give reasons for his decision unless requested in writing to do so by either party

3.6 Presumptions

The revised rent shall be the open market rent for the Demised Premises for a term of [   ] or the then unexpired residue of the Term whichever is the longer commencing on the relevant review date, on the presumption that as at that date

3.6.1   the Demised Premises is available for letting on the open market without a fine or premium with vacant possession by a willing landlord to a willing tenant

3.6.2   the Demised Premises is to be let as a whole subject to the terms of this Lease other than as to the amount of the rent

3.6.3   the Demised Premises is fit and available for immediate occupation

	3.6.4	the use of the Demised Premises is residential in accordance with the terms of this Lease
	3.6.5	the landlord's and tenant's covenants in this Lease have been fully observed and performed

Any effect on the revised rent attributable to the granting of a tenancy to a sitting tenant, any increase in value of the Demised Premises attributable to an improvement carried out by the Tenant during the Term otherwise than in pursuance of an obligation to the Landlord or in pursuance of an obligation to the Landlord that arose by reference to the consent given for that improvement and any reduction in the value of the Demised Premises attributable to a failure by the Tenant to comply with any terms of this Lease, shall be disregarded.

3.7   Time for ascertainment of the revised rent

The Valuer must try to ascertain the amount of the revised rent before the relevant review date and must ascertain it within [one month] after that date

4.   Payment of the new rent

4.1   The Tenant must continue to pay rent at the existing rate in accordance with the terms of this Lease until the revised rent is ascertained

4.2   The revised rent for any review period is to be payable from the relevant review date and must be paid until ascertainment of the rent for the next review period or as appropriate for the remainder of the Term

4.3   On ascertainment of the rent for any review period, the Tenant must forthwith pay to the Landlord the difference between the rent previously payable and the revised rent for the period from the relevant review date to the date of first payment of the revised rent [with interest at the rate of [   ]% above the base lending rate for the time being of (*name of bank*) calculated on a daily basis for that period]

5.   Memorandum of the new rent

When the rent for any review period has been ascertained in accordance with this schedule a memorandum of the amount must be endorsed on this Lease and the counterpart of it and shall be signed by or on behalf of the Landlord and the Tenant

6. Costs

The fees and expenses of any valuer appointed to act under this schedule shall be borne equally between the Landlord and the Tenant unless the valuer considers that either party has acted unreasonably in which case he may require that party to meet the whole or any part of his fees and the costs of the other party

7. Replacement of the valuer

If the Valuer appointed to ascertain the revised rent dies, refuses to act or becomes incapable of acting, or if he fails to ascertain the revised rent within (*state period*) of the date on which he accepted the appointment, then if he was appointed by agreement the parties may agree to replace him and appoint a successor. His appointment shall then cease and his successor shall act in accordance with this schedule. If the Valuer was appointed by or on behalf of the President of the Royal Institution of Chartered Surveyors either the Landlord or the Tenant may apply to the President to discharge him and appoint another valuer in his place

[6.13]

SCHEDULE 5

Insurance

5.1 Tenant's obligation to insure

The Tenant must keep the Demised Premises insured against damage or destruction by [fire, storm, tempest, earthquake, lightning, explosion, riot, civil commotion, malicious damage, terrorism, impact by vehicles and by aircraft and articles dropped from aircraft, flood damage and bursting and overflowing of water pipes and tanks (*or as required*)], and any other risks, whether or not of the same nature, that the Tenant reasonably decides to insure against from time to time ('the Insured Risks'), subject to such excesses, exclusions or limitations as the insurer requires.

5.2 Names, office and amount

Insurance must be effected [in the joint names of the Landlord, the Tenant [and any other persons the Landlord or the Tenant reasonably requires]] [in the insurance office, or with the underwriters, and through such agents as the Landlord from time to time reasonably requires (*or*) in an insurance office of repute or with underwriters] for the full cost of rebuilding and reinstating the Demised Premises, including VAT, professional fees, shoring–up, debris removal, demolition, site clearance and any works that may be required by statute, and incidental expenses, and loss of rent for [three years].

5.3   Premiums

The Tenant must pay the premium and all other payments required to maintain the insurance and produce receipts for the current premium and such payments to the Landlord on demand.

5.4   Tenant's further insurance obligations

5.4.1   The Tenant must comply with all requirements and recommendations of the insurers.

5.4.2   The Tenant must not do or omit to do anything that could cause any insurance policy effected in accordance with this Lease to become wholly or partly void or voidable.

5.4.3   The Tenant must immediately give notice to the Landlord of anything that might affect any insurance policy effected in accordance with this Lease, and of any destruction of or damage to the Demised Premises, whether or not caused by one or more of the Insured Risks.

5.4.4   The Tenant must produce to the Landlord on demand every insurance policy effected in accordance with this Lease and the receipt for the then current year's premium, and if so required must supply the Landlord with a copy of every such policy.

5.5   Reinstatement

5.5.1   Insurance money

If and whenever during the Term the Demised Premises is damaged or destroyed by one or more of the Insured Risks, all money received under the property insurance effected under this Lease must be placed in an account in the joint names of the Landlord and the Tenant to be operated by both signatures only, at a bank [approved by the Landlord, whose approval may not be unreasonably withheld or delayed, (*or*) designated by the Landlord acting reasonably]. The money may be withdrawn as necessary to pay for rebuilding and reinstating the Demised Premises as and when work is proved to have been done by architect's certificates or other evidence reasonably acceptable to the Landlord.

5.5.2 Permissions and rebuilding

The Tenant must use his best endeavours to obtain the planning permissions and other permits and consents necessary to enable the Demised Premises to be rebuilt and reinstated in accordance with the original plans, elevations and details, with any variations the Landlord agrees to, having regard to the statutory provisions, bye–laws and regulations affecting the Demised Premises. As soon as reasonably practicable after all the necessary permissions, permits and consents have been obtained, the Tenant must rebuild and reinstate the Demised Premises in accordance with them, [using new, good, sound and substantial materials that are to be subject to inspection and approval by the Landlord's surveyor, whose approval may not be unreasonably withheld or delayed,] [to the satisfaction in all respects of an independent surveyor].

5.5.3 Shortfall

The Tenant must make up out of his own money any difference between the cost of rebuilding and reinstatement and the money received from the insurance policy.

5.6 Determination on destruction

If and whenever the Demised Premises or a material part of it or the means of access to it is damaged by any risk against which it is insured so as to be unfit for occupation and use, either the Landlord or the Tenant may by written notice to the other end the Term. On expiry of the notice the Term shall end and the provisions of this Lease shall cease to have effect without prejudice to any rights or remedies that may have accrued to either party. The Tenant must pay the Rent and other payments due under this Lease up to the date of determination. The insurance money shall belong to the Landlord [and the Tenant in proportions relating to the value of their respective interests in the Demised Premises]. In default of agreement between them as to their respective entitlements the matter may be referred to an independent chartered surveyor acting as an expert. He may be appointed by agreement, or in default of agreement by or on behalf of the President for the time being of the Royal Institution of Chartered Surveyors. The expert must reach a decision within three months. His decision shall be final and binding and his costs must be paid as he awards.]

Notes to Form 6

1. Where the term will exceed seven years, it should be noted that, under the Land Registration Act 2002, s 4 a lease granted for such a term will be subject to compulsory registration.

    The rent payable under an assured shorthold tenancy or an assured tenancy is as agreed between the Landlord and the Tenant, but it should be noted that if the rent exceeds £25,000 a year it takes the tenancy out of the category of assured tenancies, and therefore assured shorthold tenancies and if the Tenant thinks that the rent is excessive he can refer it to the local rent assessment committee which, if there is a sufficient number of similar lettings and if they are satisfied that the rent charged is significantly higher than the level of rents under such lettings, may determine a rent from such date as it may direct: see the Housing Act 1988, s 22. However, the Tenant may only refer his rent to the committee during the first six months of his period of occupation.

    The periods by reference to which rent is payable are of importance if the Tenant holds over at the end of a fixed term tenancy, whether the periodic tenancy that arises is implied by the common law or by statute. Under the common law, the Tenant under a tenancy agreement for one year at a rent of £x a week who holds over becomes a weekly tenant: *Adler v Blackman* [1953] 1 QB 146, [1952] 2 All ER 945, CA. If the fixed term tenancy is an assured tenancy, at the end of the term the Tenant is entitled to remain in possession under a periodic tenancy the periods of which are the same as those for which the rent was last payable under the fixed term tenancy: see the Housing Act 1988, s 5(2),(3).

2. The periods by reference to which rent is payable are of importance if the tenant holds over at the end of a fixed-term tenancy, whether the periodic tenancy that arises is implied by the common law or by statute. Under the common law, the tenant under a tenancy agreement for one year at a rent of £x a week who holds over becomes a weekly tenant: *Adler v Blackman* [1953] 1 QB 146, [1952] 2 All ER 945, CA. If the fixed-term tenancy is an assured tenancy, at the end of the term the Tenant is entitled to remain in possession under a periodic tenancy the periods of which are the same as those for which rent was last payable under the fixed-term tenancy: see the Housing Act 1988, s 5(2), (3).

3. The rent payable under an assured shorthold tenancy or an assured tenancy is as agreed between the Landlord and the Tenant, but it should be noted that if the rent exceeds £25,000 a year it takes the tenancy out of the category of assured tenancies, and therefore assured shorthold tenancies and if the Tenant thinks that the rent is excessive he can refer it to the local rent assessment committee which, if there is a sufficient number of similar lettings and if they are satisfied that the rent charged is significantly higher than the level of rents under such lettings, may determine a rent from such date as it may direct: see the Housing Act 1988, s 22. However, the Tenant may only refer his rent to the committee during the first six months of his period of occupation.

The periods by reference to which rent is payable are of importance if the Tenant holds over at the end of a fixed term tenancy, whether the periodic tenancy that arises is implied by the common law or by statute. Under the common law, the Tenant under a tenancy agreement for one year at a rent of £x a week who holds over becomes a weekly tenant: *Adler v Blackman* [1953] 1 QB 146, [1952] 2 All ER 945, CA. If the fixed term tenancy is an assured tenancy, at the end of the term the Tenant is entitled to remain in possession under a periodic tenancy the periods of which are the same as those for which the rent was last payable under the fixed term tenancy: see the Housing Act 1988, s 5(2), (3).

4. Careful consideration should be given to rights and reservations. For example, rights relating to access, use of lifts, common areas, communal gardens etc. Reservations may be necessary, for example, to allow a right of way over a garden to access neighbouring land.

5. The operative word in a lease executed as a deed is traditionally 'demises'. In a lease not executed as a deed 'agrees to let' is commonly used. Any words sufficient to show the parties' intention may be used.

6. The *Guidance on unfair terms in tenancy agreements* (OFT 356, November 2001) says:

'Terms which limit or deprive the consumer of access to redress, as well as those which disclaim liability may be considered unfair. One legitimate way for a consumer to obtain compensation from a supplier is to exercise the right of set-off. Where a consumer has an arguable claim under the contract against a supplier, the law generally allows the amount of that claim to be deducted from anything the consumer has to pay. This helps prevent unnecessary legal proceedings.' (para 2.5.1)

'If the right of set-off is excluded, tenants may have (or believe they have) no choice but to pay their rent in full, even where they have incurred costs as a result of breach of an obligation by the landlord. To obtain redress, they then have to go to court. The costs, delays and uncertainties involved may, in practice, force them to give up their claim, and deprive them of their rights. The right of set-off should be exercised by tenants only which caution and preferably on legal advice. However, that does not justify terms which stop them from exercising it at all. The OFT does not object to terms that deter tenants from using the right of set-off to withhold excessively large sums.' (para 2.5.2, 2.5.3)

7. Use the words in square brackets where the rent is to be paid in advance, otherwise rent is taken to be payable in arrear.

8. The rate of interest should be fair. The *Guidance on unfair terms in tenancy agreements* (OFT 356, November 2001) says:

'A requirement to pay unreasonable interest on arrears of rent, for instance at a rate substantially above the clearing banks' base rates, is likely to be regarded as an unfair penalty. The tenant would have to pay more than the cost of making up the deficit caused by the tenant's default. A landlord's personal circumstances may expose him to an interest rate which would normally be considered excessive when passed on to a tenant. In this case, it may not be unfair to require tenants who default on their rent to pay a similar high rate on their arrears provided the reason for this was explained and drawn to their attention at the time of entering into the agreement.' (para 5.2)

9. The obligation to keep a property in good repair and condition are not necessarily tautologous. See the case *R v West Sussex Registration Area, ex p Haysport Properties Ltd* [2001] EWCA Civ 237, [2001] EWCA Civ 237, (2001) 33 HLR 799, (a case as to whether a new fair rent should be registered on the grounds that repairs undertaken in compliance with a repairing obligation constituted a change of condition) where it was said, obiter, that just because the Rent Act 1977 defines improvements in a way that excludes repair it does not follow that 'condition' also excludes repair. It would therefore seem that keeping in repair and keeping in condition can be two separate obligations.

10. The agreement should be tailored to ensure that the landlord has access to fulfil all his obligations as well as to check on the state of the premises, but rights of entry must not be excessive. The *Guidance on unfair terms in tenancy agreements* (OFT 356, November 2001) says:

    'A term dealing with rights of entry is unlikely to be challenged if it reflects the ordinary legal position. This recognises that a landlord who is responsible for carrying out repairs to the property needs reasonable access for two specific purposes: firstly, in order to check whether repairs are necessary, and secondly, to carry them out. Reasonable access means at reasonable times, and with reasonable notice, except in cases of urgency.' (para 2.7.5)

    The *Guidance on unfair terms in tenancy agreements* (OFT 356, November 2001) says:

    'A term that goes beyond what is reasonable is liable to be considered unfair. For example, it may be unfair to expect a tenant to comply with a repair notice immediately, regardless of particular circumstances that could make instant compliance difficult or even impossible to achieve. The general law requires contracting parties to comply with their obligations reasonably promptly.' (para 18.8.5, 3rd example).

11. The *Guidance on unfair terms in tenancy agreements* (OFT 356, November 2001) says:

    'A landlord has a legitimate interest in ensuring that his tenants do not obstruct his compliance with his obligations as a property owner, and may fairly require that they bring to his attention notices that require action on his part. But, this does not justify use of a term which could force tenants to incur trouble and costs in opposing notices which do not affect their interests, or might even (in the case of notices relating to environmental health) be designed to protect them.' (para 18.8.5, 4th example)

12. It should be remembered that, if the tenancy is an assured tenancy, when the fixed term expires a statutory periodic tenancy arises which can only be determined by the landlord on proof of one of the grounds for possession set out in the Housing Act 1988, s 7, Sch 2: see the Housing Act 1988, s 7.

13. Whether subletting should be permitted is a commercial matter, although the *Guidance on unfair terms in tenancy agreements* issued by the Office of Fair Trading in November 2001 (OFT 356) para 18.4.3 states that in a fixed term tenancy agreement an absolute ban on both assignment and subletting may be considered unfair. Some landlords consider that the fact that they cannot reasonably refuse consent to an assignment gives the tenant all the protection he requires and are not prepared to permit subletting. An advantage to the tenant of the ability to

sublet is that he has an element of control over a subtenant but not over an assignee, for whom he may retain liability under an authorised guarantee agreement. With stringent assignment tests or in a bad market, subletting may be the only option open to the tenant.

14. The right to pre-specify circumstances and conditions does not apply to any lease by which a building or part of a building is let wholly or mainly as a single private residence: see the Landlord and Tenant Act 1927, s 19(1E), (4) as inserted and amended by the Landlord and Tenant (Covenants) Act 1995, s 22. An approach that seems to have been accepted by the courts is the insertion of a clause setting out pre-conditions to the tenant's right to dispose. Care must be taken over the drafting of such provisions because under the 'old' test of reasonableness conditions purporting to prescribe circumstances in which the landlord can reasonably refuse consent are void and the court is free to decide for itself whether or not the landlord is unreasonably refusing consent: see *Creery v Summersell and Flowerdew & Co Ltd* [1949] Ch 751, *Re Smith's Lease, Smith v Richards* [1951] 1 All ER 346.

15. There are conflicting views as to the validity of this and similar covenants. One view is that it merely sets out a condition precedent that must be fulfilled before a subletting, for which consent cannot be unreasonably refused, and is thus unobjectionable: see *Bocardo SA v S and M Hotels Ltd* [1979] 3 All ER 737, [1980] 1 WLR 17, CA. The other view is that the covenant could be void under the Landlord and Tenant Act 1927, s 19(1) on the grounds that questions of reasonableness are objective ones for the court to decide without regard to the interpretations the parties have put on the expression: see *Creery v Summersell and Flowerdew & Co Ltd* [1949] Ch 751; *Re Smith's Lease, Smith v Richards* [1951] 1 All ER 346. It must be for the court to decide if in a particular case it would be reasonable for the landlord to make his licence subject to the tenant complying with the provisions of this covenant. See also *Waite v Jennings* [1906] 2 KB 11, CA and *Balfour v Kensington Garden Mansions Ltd* (1932) 49 TLR 29.

16. The words 'the Tenant paying the rents reserved by and observing and performing the covenants on his part and the conditions contained in the lease' are frequently included in a covenant for quiet enjoyment, but they have no practical effect and do not make payment of the rent and performance of the covenants into conditions precedent to the operation of the covenant for quiet enjoyment: see *Edge v Boileau* (1885) 16 QBD 117; *Dawson v Dyer* (1833) 5 B & Ad 584; *Yorkbrook Investments Ltd v Batten* (1985) 52 P & CR 51, CA.

17. The *Guidance on unfair terms in tenancy agreements* (OFT 356, November 2001) says:

> 'The law gives residential tenants considerable protection against arbitrary or immediate termination of their rights of occupation. A court order is required for eviction. The law recognises that landlords may expressly reserve the right to forfeit in the tenancy agreement. However, terms that appear to reserve a right of forfeiture or re-entry for any breach of covenant (however minor) are apt to mislead the uninformed tenant. The fact that such terms have long been extensively used does not make them fair. Forfeiture or re-entry clauses need to acknowledge the tenant's legal rights, at least in general terms, to be more acceptable. They also need to be intelligible to an ordinary person. Terms which do not make it clear that it is unlawful for a landlord to evict a tenant and re-enter the property without a court order may be open to objection. Although it may be helpful to advise the tenant to seek independent legal advice where

eviction is threatened, this will not be enough to avoid unfairness if the term does not clearly refer to the need for court proceedings.'

18. In the absence of these words a formal demand must be served.

19. It may be considered desirable to extend the events giving rise to a landlord's right of re-entry. In the case of a company tenant, the events may be extended to the making of an administration order in respect of the company, and any person becoming entitled to exercise the powers conferred on an administrative receiver: see the Insolvency Act 1986. But if the agreed rent is paid and there are no other material breaches of the lease it is difficult to see why the Landlord should be entitled to forfeit the lease on these grounds. The Insolvency Act 1986, s 10(1)(c) provides that after a petition for an administration order has been presented, no proceedings, execution or other legal process may be commenced or continued, and no distress may be levied, against the company or its property except with the leave of the court and subject, where the court gives leave, to such terms as the court may impose. The same applies after an administration order is made (see the Insolvency Act 1986, s 11(3)(d)), except that proceedings, execution and process etc may be commenced or continued with the administrator's consent. A landlord wishing to take advantage of the event will have obtain consent from the administrator or the court before commencing any proceedings or legal process. It is now clear that such consent is not required as regards as landlord's right of peaceable re-entry or distraint (see *Re a Debtor (No 13A-IO-1995)* [1996] 1 All ER 691, [1995] 1 WLR 1127) though these will rarely apply to a residential tenancy.

20. It is common for mortgages to refuse to lend on the security of a lease which contains a proviso for re-entry on the insolvency of the tenant.

21. The landlord has the option whether to take advantage of a right of forfeiture or not. If he elects not to do so, the forfeiture is waived. The election may be express or implied, e g if the landlord does any act by which he recognises that the relationship of landlord and tenant is still continuing after the cause of forfeiture has come to his knowledge.

22. The Gas Safety (Installation and Use) Regulations 1998, SI 1998/2451 relate to gas appliances in all let residential properties. All appliances must be tested by a CORGI registered engineer. A Landlord's safety certificate must be provided to the Tenant upon occupation or within 28 days of a certificate or renewal certificate being issued. It is advised that Landlords should have additional checks carried out between tenancies. Failure to comply is a criminal offence enforced by the Health and Safety Executive and conviction will result in a fine of up to £5,000 or six months' imprisonment. In addition, note that the Electrical Equipment (Safety) Regulations 1994, SI 1994/3260 provides that all electrical appliances and equipment must be tested and a portable appliance test certificate obtained, but there is no provision as to when this had be done. New electrical appliances usually have a statement as to testing. It is advised that the Landlord should have all appliances tested where it is not evident that this has been done, or re-tested, before the grant of any tenancy agreement. Non compliance could mean prosecution by the Trading Standards Office and results in a fine of up to £5,000 or six months' imprisonment.

23. Where the Law of Property Act 1925, s 62 may operate, it is sensible to define in the lease those rights that are included, and then specifically exclude the operation of that section.

24. Any term found to be unfair does not bind the tenant, but the remainder of the

tenancy continues in force provided that it is capable of continuing in existence without the unfair term: see the Unfair Terms in Consumer Contracts Regulations 1999, SI 1999/2083, reg 8(1),(2).

25. The *Guidance on unfair terms in tenancy agreements* (OFT 356, November 2001) says:

> 'Terms sometimes require the tenant to pay all the landlord's costs in bringing any court proceedings, regardless of their outcome. Under English law the award of legal costs in court proceedings is always at the discretion of the court. Such a term could be relied upon to add excessive legal costs tot he tenant's rent bill. It could also enable the landlord to seek to recover the costs of an action which a court would be likely to dismiss. A court normally awards costs against the party at fault. A term may not be open to objection if it says that the tenants who break the terms of the tenancy can expect to have to meet any reasonable legal costs properly incurred as a result.' (paras 5.9, 5.10)

26. Rent review provisions that determine the increase by reference to objective criteria or as independent valuer are not considered unfair: see the *Guidance on unfair terms in tenancy agreements* (OFT 356, November 2001) (para 12.2):

> 'Terms which permit increases linked to a relevant published price index outside the Landlord's control, such as the RPI, are likely to be acceptable, on paragraph 2(d) of Schedule 2 to the Regulations indicates.' (para 12.4)

> 'Also likely to be fair are rent review clauses which allow for an increase in the rent to be determined in the light of objective factors by a person who is independent of the Landlord. A fair alternative, where the parties cannot agree a new rent, is to agree that the matter should be referred to an independent expert' (para 12.4)

Form 7
Tenancy agreement for a holiday letting[1]

(a table of contents may usefully be made from the clause, subclause, schedule and paragraph headings, with or without page numbers)

TAKE NOTICE THAT THIS TENANCY AGREEMENT IS A BINDING DOCUMENT. BEFORE SIGNING IT YOU SHOULD READ IT CAREFULLY TO ENSURE THAT IT CONTAINS EVERYTHING YOU DO WANT AND NOTHING UNACCEPTABLE TO YOU[2].

THIS AGREEMENT is made on [   ] BETWEEN

(1) *[name of landlord]* [of *[address]* (*or*) whose registered office is at *[address]*, company registration number [   ]] ('the Landlord')

(2) *[name of tenant]* of *[address]* ('the Tenant')

[7.1]

1. Particulars

[1.1 **'the Agents'** *[name]* of *[address]*]]

[1.2 **'the Building'** means the [building (*or*) block of flats] known as *[address]* of which the Property forms part, including any common parts, forecourts, parking areas, gardens and land held with it;]

1.3 **'the Contents'** means the furniture, fittings and effects set out in the inventory annexed to this agreement [which states both the individual items and their present condition,] , copies of which have been signed by [the Agents on behalf of] the Landlord and by the Tenant, which are let with the Property under this agreement;

1.4 **'the Deposit'** means £[   ]

1.2 **'the Property'** means The [house (*or*) flat on the ... floor of the Building (*or as required*)] known as *[insert postal address]* [shown [for the purpose of identification only] edged [red] on the plan annexed to this agreement] with the rights for the Tenant set out in Schedule 1 and the rights for the Landlord set out in Schedule 2.

1.3 **'the Rent'** means £[   ] a [year (*or*) month];

[1.4 **'the Term'** means [2] [weeks (*or*) months] from and including (*date*).]

[7.2]

2. Interpretation

2.1   Where the Landlord or the Tenant for the time being comprises two or more persons, obligations expressed or implied to be made by or with them are deemed to be made by or with such persons jointly and severally.

2.2   Words importing one gender include all other genders, words importing the singular include the plural and vice versa, and words importing persons shall be construed as importing a corporate body or a partnership and vice versa.

2.3   References in this agreement to any clause, subclause or schedule without further designation shall be construed as a reference to the clause, subclause or schedule to this agreement so numbered.

2.4   The clause, paragraph and schedule headings do not form part of this agreement and shall not be taken into account in its construction or interpretation.

[7.3]

3. Holiday Letting

This agreement is made on the basis that the Property is to be occupied by the Tenant for a holiday[3] as mentioned in the Housing Act 1988, Schedule 1, Paragraph 9. The Tenant acknowledges that the tenancy granted by this agreement is not an assured tenancy and that no statutory periodic tenancy will arise on the determination of the Term.

[7.4]

4. Letting

The Landlord lets and the Tenant takes the Property and the Contents for the Term at the Rent [with the rights for the Tenant set out in Schedule 1 [and excepting and reserving the rights for the Landlord set out in Schedule 2]].

[7.5]

5. Rent

The Tenant must pay the Rent [together with any VAT for which the landlord is accountable][4] to the Landlord in advance [commencing on] [*date*].

[7.6]

6. Outgoings

6.1 Tenant

The Tenant must pay all charges for gas and electric current supplied to the Property during the Term, any charge for gas or electricity supplied partly during and partly before or after the Term being apportioned.

6.2 Landlord

The Landlord must pay all the water and sewerage charges and any rates or taxes levied in respect of the Property.

[7.7]

7. Protection of the Property

7.1 Alterations

The Tenant must not make any alterations or additions to the Property or its decorations, fixtures or fittings, or the Contents.

7.2 Defacement

The Tenant must not deface the Property or permit or suffer it to be defaced internally or externally.

7.3 Contents

The Tenant must keep the Contents in its present state of repair and condition and replace with similar articles of at least equal value any articles that are found to be missing or destroyed or so damaged as to be incapable of being restored to their former condition, reasonable wear and tear and damage by accidental fire excepted. The Tenant must not move any items of furniture from room to room in the Property and must replace in its original position any furniture that is moved within rooms[5].

[7.4 Windows

The Tenant must keep the internal [and external] surfaces of all windows of the Property clean.]

[7.5   Garden

The Tenant must keep the grass and hedges on the Property cut and trimmed and the pathways weeded and the beds in a fit state of cultivation and not overgrown with weeds, and clear away fallen leaves.]

[7.8]

8.   Use and Nuisance

8.1   Use

The Tenant must use the Property for the purpose of a private holiday residence for a maximum of [4] persons only and not for any other purpose whatsoever.

8.2   Advertisements

The Tenant must not fix or exhibit any placard, poster or other advertisement on any part of the outside of the Property, or allow anyone else to do so.

8.3   Nuisance

The Tenant must not do anything on or in connection with the Property that may be or tend to be a nuisance, annoyance or cause of damage to the Landlord or to any neighbouring or adjoining property or its owners or occupiers, or allow anyone else to do so.

8.4   Illegal or immoral purpose

The Tenant must not use the Property or any part of it for any illegal or immoral[6] purpose, or allow anyone else to do so.

8.5   Noise

The Tenant must not play any musical instrument or device and must not allow noise from a radio, television set, compact disc, tape or record player or sound production system of any kind or any machine or equipment to be heard outside the Property after 2300 hours or before 0800 hours.

8.6   Drains

The Tenant must not block the sinks, baths, lavatories, cisterns or pipes in the Property with rags, dirt, rubbish, refuse or other substances, and must not cause any obstruction or blockage in the sinks, baths, lavatories, cisterns or pipes or damage them in any other way.

[7.9]

9. Underletting

The Tenant must not assign, underlet or part with or share possession[7] of the Property or any part of it[8].

[7.10]

10. Entry and Repairs

10.1 Right of entry

The Tenant must permit the Landlord to enter the Property at all reasonable times with all necessary workmen and appliances, upon giving 24 hours notice except in case of emergency:

[(*insert reasons for entry as required, e g:*)

10.1.1 to inspect the Property and the Contents;

10.1.2 to carry out any repairs [or alterations] that may be necessary during the Term pursuant to the Landlord's repairing obligations[9];

10.1.3 to carry out any repairs[, alterations, or improvements] to the Property or the electric wiring, gas or water pipes or drains in or under the Property;

10.1.4 to execute all work necessary to remedy the Tenant's breach of any covenant contained in this agreement regarding repair, maintenance or decoration[10];

10.1.5 to paint the outside of the Property [or the Building]; and

10.1.6 to make inventories of all fixtures on the Property.]

10.2 Inspection and reporting

The Tenant must inspect the Property regularly for any defect or disrepair in the Property or in any installation in it for which the Landlord is responsible, and if any is found report it to the Landlord in writing as soon as possible.

[7.11]

11. Deposit

11.1 Payment

The Tenant must pay the Deposit shown in the Particulars to the Landlord with the Rent, to be held by the Landlord until the end of the Term as security towards the Tenant's liability for gas and electricity accounts, telephone rental and charges and dilapidations and any other sums that may be due from the Tenant to the Landlord under this agreement.

11.2 Repayment

The Landlord acknowledges receipt of the Deposit from the Tenant and agrees to repay it to the Tenant at the end of the Term less any sum that may be due to the Landlord from the Tenant as a result of any breach of the Tenant's agreements.

[7.12]

12. End of the Term

12.1 Delivery

The Tenant must deliver up the Property and the Contents at the end of the Term clean tidy and in accordance with the provisions of this agreement.

[7.13]

13. Quiet Enjoyment

The Landlord must permit the Tenant peaceably to hold and enjoy the Property during the Term without any interruption or disturbance from or by the Landlord or any person claiming under or in trust for him.

[7.14]

14. Insurance

14.1 Landlord's obligation to insure

The Landlord must keep the Property and the Contents insured at all times throughout the Term against loss or damage by fire and any other risks he decides to insure against from time to time in his absolute discretion, in some insurance office of repute for the full cost of reinstatement.

14.2 Tenant's obligations

The Tenant must not do anything or allow anything to be done as a result of which the Landlord's insurance on the Property may become void or voidable or as a result of which the rate of premium on the policy may be increased.

14.3 Suspension of rent

If the Property or any part of it is damaged or destroyed by fire so as to be unfit for habitation and use, the Rent or a fair proportion of it according to the nature and extent of the damage sustained shall be suspended until the Property is fit for habitation and use again. If the rent for the period of suspension has been paid in advance the Landlord must repay it or a fair proportion of it to the Tenant.

[7.15]

15. Re-entry

If at any time during the Term:

15.1. the Rent or any part of it is unpaid for [*number*] days after becoming payable, whether formally demanded or not[11], or

15.2 any covenant by the Tenant contained in this lease is not performed or observed, or

15.3 the Property is left unoccupied for more than [*number*] days continuously otherwise than by prior agreement with the Landlord

the Landlord may at any time after that re-enter upon the Property or any part of it in the name of the whole. Upon re-entry this tenancy shall end but without prejudice to the right of action of the Landlord in respect of any breach of any covenant by the Tenant contained in this agreement[12].

[7.16]

16. Safety Regulations

16.1 Fire safety

The Landlord confirms that all furniture and furnishings comply with the Furniture and Furnishings (Fire) (Safety) Regulations 1988 as amended[13].

16.2 Gas safety

[The Landlord has (*or*) The Agents have] complied with the Gas Safety (Installation and Use) Regulations 1998 and an appropriate Gas Safety Certificate is available at [his (*or*) their] address for inspection by the Tenant[14].

16.3 Electrical safety

The Landlord confirms that all electrical appliances and equipment supplied by him are safe so as not to cause danger and all electrical appliances and equipment manufactured since 19 January 1977 are marked with the appropriate CE symbol[15].

[7.17]

17. Notices

Any notice to be given in connection with the Term shall be deemed to be properly given if delivered by hand or sent by registered post or recorded delivery addressed:

    17.1   if given to the Landlord or the Agent, to him by name at the address stated to be his address in this agreement, and

    17.2   if given to the Tenant, to him by name at the address of the Property.

Any notice sent by post shall be deemed to have been served not later than the first working day following the day on which it was posted.

[AS (*or*) IN] WITNESS etc (*see vol 12 (1994 Reissue) DEEDS, AGREE-MENTS AND DECLARATIONS Form 90 [1691] et seq*)

[7.18]

SCHEDULE 1

The rights granted

The Property is let together with the following rights:

[insert rights as required, eg access, car parking, services, support and protection, entry for repairs][16]

[7.19]

SCHEDULE 2

Rights excepted and reserved

The Property is let subject to the following exceptions and reservations reserved for the benefit of the Landlord's adjoining premises and every part of them:

[insert reservations as required, eg services, construction of conduits, support and shelter, erection of scaffolding][17]

[signatures (or common seals) of the parties]

Notes to Form 7
*   This Form was originally published in Volume 23(2) of the Encyclopedia of Forms and Precedents.
1.   As to stamp duty see the Information Binder: Stamp Duties [1] (Lease or Tack) and (Duplicate or Counterpart). A tenancy the purpose of which is to confer on the tenant the right to occupy a dwelling house for a holiday cannot be an assured tenancy: see the Housing Act 1988, s 1, Sch 1, para 9 (23 *Halsbury's Statutes* (4th Edn) LANDLORD AND TENANT). A holiday letting is an excluded tenancy for the purposes of the Protection from Eviction Act 1977 (23 Halsbury's Statutes (4th Edn) LANDLORD AND TENANT): see the Protection from Eviction Act 1977, s 3A(7) as inserted by the Housing Act 1988, s 31. The question of whether a tenancy is for a holiday is one of fact, to be decided according to the substance of the transaction and not merely any label which the parties may attach to it: *Facchini v Bryson* (1952) 96 Sol Jo 395, CA. For a form of licence to occupy property for a holiday see vol 23(1) (2002 Reissue) LANDLORD AND TENANT (RESIDEN-TIAL TENANCIES) Form 6 [1545].

It seems that the Unfair Terms in Consumer Contracts Regulations 1999, SI 1999/2083 will apply and, therefore, that the *Guidance on unfair terms in tenancy agreements* (OFT 356, November 2001) is relevant.

2.   See the *Guidance on unfair terms in tenancy agreements* (OFT 356, November 2001) para 14.1.5:

'Such a warning can strengthen written terms, provided that tenants are genuinely likely to see, understand and act on it. If this is the case, there is less scope for misunderstanding, and thus less likelihood of plausible allegations that oral statements were relied on. However, the warning needs to be sufficiently highlighted in some way in order to draw it to the tenant's attention. Moreover, the agreement must be drafted in plain intelligible language, or the tenant will be unable to spot a potential contradiction between what is said and what is printed.' (para 14.1.6)

3. Where a tenancy agreement expressly states the purpose for which it is made, that statement is evidence of the purpose of the parties unless the tenant can establish that it does not correspond with the true purpose: *Buchmann v May* [1978] 2 All ER 993, CA.

4. The letting of holiday accommodation is a standard rated supply for VAT purposes: see the Value Added Tax Act 1994, Sch 9, Part II, Group I, Item 1(e) (50 Halsbury's Statutes (4th Edn) VALUE ADDED TAX). If the landlord is registered or liable to be registered for VAT he must charge VAT on the amount of the rent.

5. It is common to forbid all movement of furniture. However, the *Guidance on unfair terms in tenancy agreements* (OFT 356, November 2001) says:

    'The risk of damage to, or of difficulties in restoring the property to its previous state at the end of the tenancy, may make it fair to forbid tenants to move fixtures, or bulky or fragile furniture. However, it cannot be reasonable for tenants to be prohibited from moving furniture, such as chairs.' (para 18.8.5, 6th example)

6. 'Immoral' is not confined to prostitution (*London Scottish Properties v Mehmet* (1970) 214 Estates Gazette 837), but does not include unmarried couples living together (*Heglibiston Establishments v Heyman* (1977) 36 P & CR 351).

7. A covenant not to assign or underlet without the addition of a prohibition on parting with possession does not prohibit an equitable assignment: see *Gentle v Faulkner* [1900] 2 QB 267, CA. A licence to use part of the premises does not constitute an underletting because it does not confer any estate or interest in land: see *Jackson v Simons* [1923] 1 Ch 373. A covenant not to part with possession is much wider but is broken only if the tenant entirely excludes himself from the legal possession of the whole or part of the premises: *Jackson v Simons* (above), and, therefore, sharing possession should also be excluded.

8. A covenant not to assign or sublet does not prevent assigning or subletting of part of the premises (*Cook v Shoesmith* [1951] 1 KB 752), therefore the point should be covered expressly.

9. It is an implied term of every assured tenancy that the tenant must afford to the landlord access to the dwelling house let on the tenancy and all reasonable facilities for executing in it any repairs the landlord is entitled to execute: see the Housing Act 1988, s 16. As this tenancy cannot be assured, the point must be covered expressly. The *Guidance on unfair terms in tenancy agreements* (OFT 356, November 2001) states that a term allowing the landlord discretion to alter the building or remove or change its furniture, during the currency of the tenancy agreement, is likely to be unfair. A term that allows the landlord to vary what he supplies should be clearly restricted to minor technical adjustments that do not disadvantage the tenant, or to changes required by law: see para 11.2.

10. If no power of entry to carry out repairs rendered necessary by the tenant's default is reserved, the landlord will be a trespasser if he enters to carry out such repairs: *Hamilton v Martell Securities Ltd* [1984] Ch 266, [1984] 1 All ER 665.

11. In the absence of these words a formal demand must be served.

12. The landlord has a right of action for existing breaches of covenant even without this express provision: *Hartshorne v Watson* (1838) 4 Bing NC 178; *Blore v Giulini* [1903] 1 KB 356.

13. The Furniture and Furnishings (Fire) (Safety) Regulations 1988, SI 1988/1324 as amended by SI 1993/207 provide that where furniture or furnishings are supplied 'in the course of business' (but even domestic owners who have never granted a

tenancy before are likely to be doing so 'as a business' unless the letting is to a family member) must ensure that such furniture etc complies with the regulations as to fire retardant materials. The covers and the fillings or anything upholstered or which has filling material e g beds, mattresses, headboards, sofas and chairs fitted with loose covers, futons, cushions and pillows, garden furniture and nursery furniture are within the regulations. Items manufactured before 1950, carpets, curtains, duvets and loose covers for mattresses are outside the regulations. Compliance can be proved by manufacturer's labels, receipts for purchase or certificates by interior designers. Failure to comply can result in prosecution by the Trading Standards Office and conviction can result in a fine of up to £5,000 or six months' imprisonment.

14. The Gas Safety (Installation and Use) Regulations 1998, SI 1998/2451 relate to gas appliances in all let residential properties. All appliances must be tested by a CORGI registered engineer. A landlord's safety certificate must be provided to the tenant upon occupation or within 28 days of a certificate or renewal certificate being issued. It is advised that landlords should have additional checks carried out between tenancies. Failure to comply is a criminal offence enforced by the Health and Safety Executive and conviction will result in a fine of up to £5,000 or six months' imprisonment.

15. The Electrical Equipment (Safety) Regulations 1994, SI 1994/3260 provides that all electrical appliances and equipment must be tested and a portable appliance test certificate obtained, but there is no provision as to when this has to be done. New electrical appliances usually have a statement as to testing. It is advised that the landlord should have all appliances tested where it is not evident that this has been done, or re-tested, before the grant of any tenancy agreement. Non compliance could mean prosecution by the Trading Standards Office and results in a fine of up to £5,000 or six months' imprisonment.

16. For examples of rights granted see Form 113 [2271] et seq post and vol 13(1) (1996 Reissue) EASEMENTS AND PROFITS À PRENDRE Form 13 [5601] et seq.

17. For examples of reservations see Form 113 [2271] et seq post and vol 13(1) (1996 Reissue) EASEMENTS AND PROFITS À PRENDRE Form 13 [5601] et seq.

Form 8
Tenancy agreement for a garage[1]

(a table of contents may usefully be made from the clause, subclause, schedule and paragraph headings, with or without page numbers)

THIS AGREEMENT is made on [   ] BETWEEN

(1) [*name of landlord*] [of [*address*] (*or*) whose registered office is at [*address*], company registration number [   ] ('the Landlord')

(2) [*name of tenant*] of [*address*] ('the Tenant')

[8.1]

1. Definitions and Interpretation

1.1 **'the Property'** means the building used as a garage situated at (*address or description*) [and shown edged (*colour*) on the plan annexed to this agreement].

1.2 **'the Rent'** means £[   ] a [month (*or*) week] [exclusive of VAT (if any)][2].

[1.3 **'the Insurance Rent'** means sums equal to the premiums for insuring the Property paid by the Landlord from time to time, including any increased premium payable by reason of any act or omission by the Tenant.]

[1.4 **'the Total Rent'** means the Rent plus the Insurance Rent.]

[*insert other definitions if required*]

1.5 Wherever the context so admits, the expression 'the Landlord' includes the person for the time being entitled to the reversion immediately expectant on the determination of the Term.

1.6 The expression 'the Tenant' [as this agreement excludes the Tenant's ability to assign or sublet,] includes the Tenant's [successor in title] personal representatives, administrator or trustee in bankruptcy only.

1.7 Where the Landlord or the Tenant for the time being comprises two or more persons, obligations expressed or implied to be made by or with them are deemed to be made by or with such persons jointly and severally.

1.8   Words importing one gender include all other genders, words importing the singular include the plural and vice versa, and words importing persons shall be construed as importing a corporate body or a partnership and vice versa.

1.9   References in this agreement to any clause, subclause or schedule without further designation shall be construed as a reference to the clause, subclause or schedule to this agreement so numbered.

1.10   The clause, paragraph and schedule headings do not form part of this agreement and shall not be taken into account in its construction or interpretation.

[8.2]

2.   Agreement to Let

The Landlord agrees to let and the Tenant agrees to take the Property [with the rights for the Tenant set out in Schedule 1 [and excepting and reserving the rights for the Landlord set out in Schedule 2],] for the term of [one month] beginning on and including [*date*] and ending on [*date*] and thereafter from month to month until determined by notice, at the [Total] Rent [subject to the following agreements, rights, easements and covenants to which the Property is subject [*insert details*]].]

[8.3]

3.   Agreements

The Tenant and the Landlord mutually agree to observe the requirements in this agreement.

[8.4]

4.   Rent [and Insurance Rent]

4.1   Rent

The Tenant must pay the Rent by equal [monthly (*or*) weekly] payments in [advance (*or*) arrears] on (*state days for payment*). The first payment [being a proportionate part of the [monthly (*or*) weekly] payment] must be made on [*date*].

[4.2   Insurance rent

The Tenant must, by way of further rent, pay the Insurance Rent once a year on [*date*].]

[8.5]

5. Outgoings

The Tenant must pay the rates, taxes assessments and outgoings imposed or charged on the Property or on the owner or occupier of it during this tenancy.

[8.6]

6. Repair

6.1 Landlord's obligations

The Landlord must keep the outside of the Property, except the glass, and the floor, walls and main timbers of the Property in tenantable repair.

6.2 Tenant's obligations

The Tenant must keep in tenantable repair all windows and skylights, doors, locks, hinges, bolts, latches, fasteners and water pipes, and the interior of the Property and all additions to it, except for damage by any risk against which the Property is insured by the Landlord unless the insurance has been wholly or partly invalidated by any act or default of the Tenant or anyone under his control.

6.3 Decoration

The Tenant must clean down and paint all the previously painted inside wood and iron work as and when necessary with suitable good quality paint, and must clean down the interior of the Property other than the wood and iron work and paint any parts previously painted with suitable paint as and when necessary.

[8.7]

7. Entry and Notice to Repair

The Tenant must permit the Landlord or his duly authorised agent, with or without workmen, to enter upon and examine the condition of the Property at all reasonable times during this tenancy after giving [24 hours'] prior notice. After each inspection the Landlord may serve upon the Tenant notice in writing that specifies any repairs needing to be done and requires the Tenant to execute them as soon as practicable. If the Tenant does not commence the repairs and proceed diligently with them within a reasonable time after service of the notice, the Landlord may enter the Property and execute the specified repairs. The cost of them shall be a debt due from the Tenant to the Landlord and be recoverable by an action.

[8.8]

8. Alterations

The Tenant must not make structural or other alterations to the Property [without the Landlord's written consent].

[8.9]

9. Dealings

The Tenant must not assign, underlet or part with the possession of the Property or any part of it [without the written consent of the Landlord].

[8.10]

10. Use

The Tenant must not use the Property for the purpose of any trade or business, but as a private garage only.

[8.11]

11. Storage of Petrol, etc

The Tenant must observe all statutory provisions and all provisions contained in regulations made by any duly constituted authority or in any policy of insurance relating to the Property with regard to the storage and use of petrol and other explosive or inflammatory oils or substances.

[8.12]

12. End of the Tenancy

At the end of this tenancy the Tenant must yield up the Property and all fixtures on and additions to it except tenant's fixtures, in tenantable repair in accordance with the Tenant's covenants contained in this agreement.

[insert any other agreements by the tenant that are required]

[8.13]

13 Quiet Enjoyment

The Landlord must permit the Tenant peaceably to hold and enjoy the Property during the tenancy created by this agreement without any interruption or disturbance from or by the Landlord or any person claiming under or in trust for him.

[8.14]

14 Re-entry

If at any time during this tenancy:

14.1 the [Total] Rent or any part of it is unpaid for [14] days after becoming payable, whether formally demanded or not,

14.2 any of the Tenant's obligations contained in this agreement are not performed or observed,

14.3 an interim receiver is appointed in respect of the Tenant's property, a bankruptcy order is made in respect of the Tenant, or the Tenant makes any arrangement with his creditors or suffers any distress or execution to be levied on his goods,

14.4 the Tenant, being a company, enters into liquidation, whether compulsory or voluntary, save for the purpose of reconstruction or amalgamation, or

14.5 the Tenant enters into any composition with his creditors or suffers any distress or execution to be levied on his goods,

the Landlord may at any time after that re-enter upon the Property and this tenancy shall end, but without prejudice to the right of action of the Landlord in respect of any antecedent breach of the Tenant's obligations under it.

[8.15]

15. Insurance

15.1 The Landlord's obligation to insure

The Landlord must insure the Property, but not the Tenant's personal property, with an insurance company of repute against [fire, lightning, explosion, aircraft (including articles dropped from aircraft), riots, civil commotion, malicious persons, earthquake, storm, tempest, flood, bursting and overflowing of water pipes, tanks and other apparatus, impact by road vehicles (*or as required*)] and any other risks he decides to insure against from time to time in his absolute discretion.

15.2 The Tenant's obligations

The Tenant must not do anything or allow anything to be done as a result of which the insurance on the Property may become void or voidable or increase the rate of premium, and must reimburse the Landlord for any costs arising from a breach of this obligation.

15.3 Suspension of rent

If at any time during this tenancy the Property or any part of it is destroyed or damaged by any risk against which it is insured so that it is unfit for use as a garage, the [Total] Rent or a fair proportion of it according to the nature and extent of the damage shall be suspended until the Property is fit for use. Any dispute concerning this clause may be determined by a single arbitrator in accordance with the Arbitration Act 1996 or any statutory modification or re-enactment of it from time to time.

[insert rent review provision if required]

[AS (*or*) IN] WITNESS etc (see vol 12 (1994 Reissue) DEEDS, AGREEMENTS AND DECLARATIONS Form 90 [1691] et seq)

SCHEDULE 1

The rights granted

The Property is let together with the following rights:

[insert rights as required, e g access, car parking, services, support and protection, entry for repairs][3]

SCHEDULE 2

Rights excepted and reserved

The Property is let subject to the following exceptions and reservations reserved for the benefit of the Landlord's adjoining premises and every part of them:

[insert reservations as required, e g services, construction of conduits, support and shelter, erection of scaffolding]*[4]*

[signatures (or common seals) of the parties]

Notes to Form 8
*   This Form was originally published in Volume 23(2) of the Encyclopedia of Forms and Precedents.
1.   As to stamp duty see the Information Binder: Stamp Duties [1]: Table of Duties (Lease) and (Duplicate or Counterpart).
2.   VAT: the supply of facilities for parking a vehicle is standard-rated. If the landlord is registered or liable to be registered for VAT he should charge VAT on the amount of the rent: see the Value Added Tax Act 1994, Sch 9, Part II, Group I, Item 1(h) (50 Halsbury's Statutes (4th edn) VALUE ADDED TAX).
3.   For examples of rights granted see Form 113 [2271] et seq post and vol 13(1) (1996 Reissue) EASEMENTS AND PROFITS À PRENDRE Form 13 [5601] et seq.
4.   For examples of reservations see Form 113 [2271] et seq post and vol 13(1) (1996 Reissue) EASEMENTS AND PROFITS À PRENDRE Form 13 [5601] et seq.

Form 9
Licence to occupy a car parking space

(A table of contents may usefully be made from the clause, subclause, schedule and paragraph headings, with or without page numbers)

THIS AGREEMENT is made on [   ] BETWEEN
(1) [*name of owner*] [of [*address*] (*or*) whose registered office is at [*address*], company registration number [   ]] ('the Owner')
(2) [*name of tenant*] of [*address*] ('the User')

NOW IT IS AGREED as follows:

[9.1]

1. Definitions
In this agreement:
1.1 'the Car' means the private motor [car (*or*) van [*or as the case may be*]] number [   ]; and
1.2 'the Property' means the [car park (*or*) block of garages [*or as the case may be*]] at [*address*] [shown edged red on the plan annexed to this agreement].

[9.2]

2. Agreement
The Owner gives the User permission to park the Car [in (*or*) on] the Property.

[9.3]

3. Consideration
The User must pay to the Owner the sum of £[   ] on [*state days for payment*]. The first payment must be made on [*date*].

[9.4]

4. Allocation of Space
The User must park the Car in the [parking space (*or*) lock-up unit] comprised in the Property that the Owner at his sole discretion from time to

time allocates to the User for his use. The allocation may be changed by the Owner without previous notice as often as he thinks fit and nothing in this agreement shall be construed as conferring on the User any exclusive right to use of any particular [space (*or*) unit] in the Property.

[9.5]

[5. Keys and Security Devices

The Owner must at all times during the subsistence of this licence supply and the User must use a key or security device allowing access to the part of the Property on which he is for the time being directed by the Owner to park the Car.]

[9.6]

6. Nuisance

The User must not run the engine of the Car whilst it is on the Property except as necessary for entering or leaving the Property and proceeding to or departing from the [parking space (*or*) garage] for the time being allocated to him, and must not do anything on or in the Property that may cause a nuisance, discomfort or annoyance to the Owner or any occupant of nearby premises, or allow anyone under his control to do so.

[9.7]

7. Restrictions on Petrol

The User must not take onto or keep at the Property any petrol, diesel or lubricating oil other than that in the tank and engine of the Car [except for any quantity of petrol or oil the Owner expressly permits the User to store in containers approved by the Owner].

[9.8]

8. Fire precautions and Damage

The User must take all reasonable and proper precautions to prevent fire occurring on or in the Property. The User must indemnify the Owner against all damage to the Property or anything for the time being in the Property belonging to a third party that results from the use, movement or presence of the Car on the Property [and must cover his liabilities under this clause by an adequate policy of insurance].

[insert other tenant's obligations as required]

[9.9]

9. Owner's Liability

The Owner must keep [the structure of] the Property [weatherproof and] safe for use by the User, but frost precautions are the responsibility of the User. The Owner does not accept any responsibility for the entry of unauthorised persons into the Property or for any loss or damage occasioned by such persons.

[9.10]

10. Determination

This agreement shall continue until terminated by one [week's (*or*) month's] written notice given by either party to the other.

AS WITNESS etc (see vol 12 (1994 Reissue) DEEDS, AGREEMENTS AND DECLARATIONS Form 90 [1691] et seq)

[signatures (or common seals) of the parties]

Note to Form 9

* This Form was originally published in Volume 23(2) of the Encyclopedia of Forms and Precedents.

Index

All entries refer to page number.